D1490239

Hiking South Florida and the Keys

A Guide to 39 Great Walking and Hiking Adventures

M. Timothy O'Keefe

FALCONGUIDES ®

GUILFORD, CONNECTICUT
HELENA, MONTANA
AN IMPRINT OF THE GLOBE PEQUOT PRESS

FALCONGUIDES®

Copyright © 2009 by Morris Book Publishing, LLC

ALL RIGHTS RESERVED. No part of this book may be reproduced or transmitted in any form by any means, electronic or mechanical, including photocopying and recording, or by any information storage and retrieval system, except as may be expressly permitted in writing from the publisher. Requests for permission should be addressed to The Globe Pequot Press, Attn: Rights and Permissions Department, P.O. Box 480, Guilford, CT 06437.

Falcon and FalconGuides are registered trademarks and Outfit Your Mind is a trademark of Morris Book Publishing, LLC.

Text design by Nancy Freeborn
Maps created by Trailhead Graphics, Inc. © Morris Book Publishing, LLC
All interior photos © M. Timothy O'Keefe

Library of Congress Cataloging-in-Publication Data

O'Keefe, M. Timothy.
  Hiking south Florida and the Keys : a guide to 39 great walking and hiking adventures / M. Timothy O'Keefe.
    p. cm. – (Falconguides)
  ISBN 978-0-7627-4355-1
  1. Hiking—Florida–Guidebooks. 2. Hiking—Florida—Florida Keys—Guidebooks. 3. Walking—Florida—Guidebooks. 4. Walking—Florida—Florida Keys—Guidebooks. 5. Florida—Guidebooks. 6. Florida Keys (Fla.)—Guidebooks. 7. Canoes and canoeing—Florida—Florida Keys—Guidebooks. I. Title.
  GV199.42.F6056 2009
  917.594104'64–dc22
                              2008042754

Printed in the United States of America

10 9 8 7 6 5 4 3 2 1

3 4015 06986 2751

To buy books in quantity for corporate use
or incentives, call **(800) 962–0973**
or e-mail **premiums@GlobePequot.com.**

The author and The Globe Pequot Press assume no liability for accidents happening to, or injuries sustained by, readers who engage in the activities described in this book.

For Linda, and all the mosquito bites we have shared together

HELP US KEEP THIS GUIDE UP TO DATE

Every effort has been made by the author and editors to make this guide as accurate and useful as possible. However, many things can change after a guide is published—trails are rerouted, regulations change, techniques evolve, facilities come under new management, etc.

We welcome your comments concerning your experiences with this guide and how you feel it could be improved and kept up to date. While we may not be able to respond to all comments and suggestions, we'll take them to heart, and we'll also make certain to share them with the author. Please send your comments and suggestions to the following address:

The Globe Pequot Press
Reader Response/Editorial Department
P.O. Box 480
Guilford, CT 06437

Or you may e-mail us at: editorial@GlobePequot.com

Thanks for your input, and happy trails!

Contents

Acknowledgments xi
Preface xii
Introduction 1
    What You'll See 1
    Archaeology and History 3
    The Everglades 3
    What to Avoid Outdoors 6
    Florida Trail Association 10
    Florida State Parks 11
    Hiking Techniques 12
    Hiking with Children 12
    How to Use This Guide 13
Trail Finder Chart 14
Map Legend 17

The Hikes
Short Family Walks
Myakka River State Park
  1 Canopy Walkway and Boylston Nature Trail 19
Highlands Hammock State Park
  2 Nature Trails 24
Six Mile Cypress Slough Preserve
  3 Boardwalk Trail 31
Corkscrew Swamp Sanctuary
  4 Boardwalk Trail 35
Florida Panther National Wildlife Refuge
  5 Duncan Memorial Trail 39
Fakahatchee Strand Preserve State Park
  6 Nature Boardwalk 44
Everglades National Park: Hikes along the Main Road 48
  7 Royal Palm Hike: Anhinga Trail 50
  8 Royal Palm Hike: Gumbo Limbo Trail 53
  9 Pinelands Short Loop 55
  10 Pa-Hay-Okee Overlook Trail 56
  11 Mahogany Hammock Trail 58
  12 West Lake Mangrove Trail 60
  13 Eco Pond Trail 63
  14 Bayshore Loop Trail 64
  15 Shark Valley: Bobcat Boardwalk and Otter Cave Hammock Trail 66
Loxahatchee National Wildlife Refuge
  16 Cypress Swamp Boardwalk 69
J. W. Corbett Wildlife Management Area
  17 Hungryland Boardwalk and Trail 73

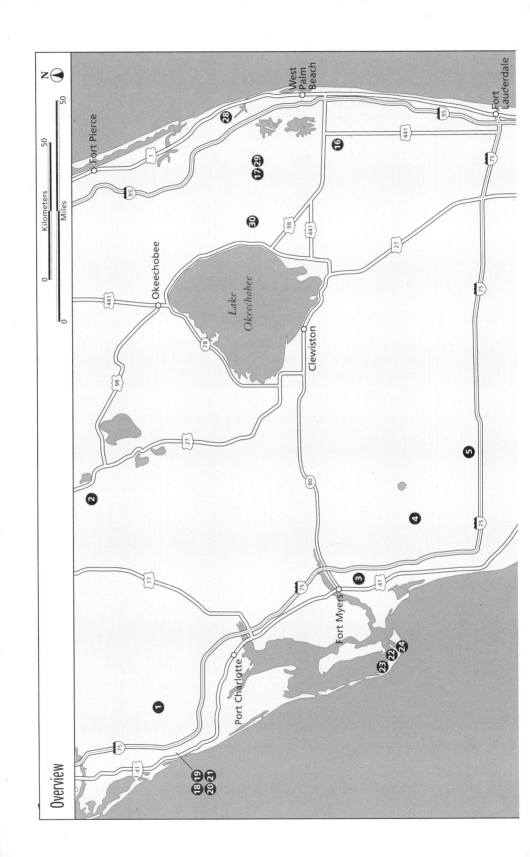

Overview

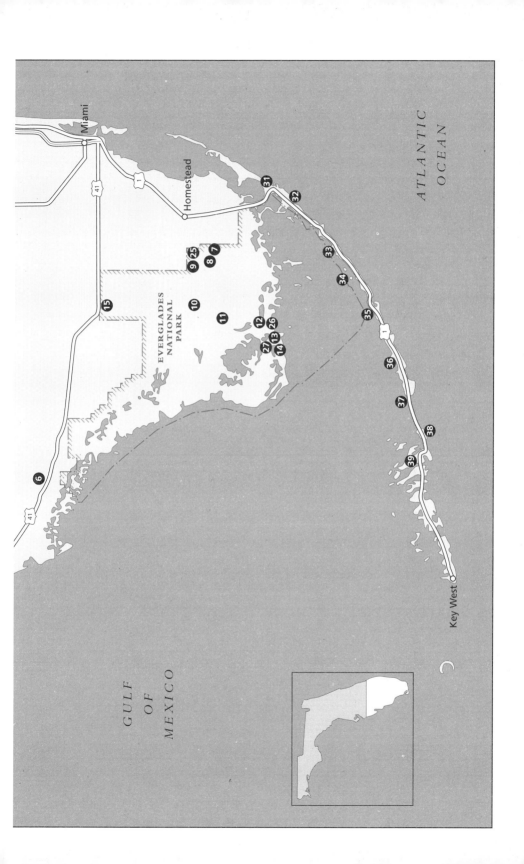

Day and Overnight Hikes

Oscar Scherer State Park... 78
   18 Yellow Trail 80
   19 Blue Trail 82
   20 Red Trail 84
   21 Green Trail.. 86
Ding Darling National Wildlife Refuge 87
   22 Indigo Trail 89
   23 Shell Mound Trail 92
   24 Bailey Tract 94
Everglades National Park: Homestead to Flamingo Day Hikes.............. 95
   25 Pinelands Long Loop 97
   26 Snake Bight/Rowdy Bend Trails 100
   27 Bear Lake Trail 102

Long Haulers

Jonathan Dickinson State Park
   28 East Loop Trail 105
J. W. Corbett Wildlife Management Area
   29 Florida Trail Segment 110
DuPuis Management Area
   30 Loop Trails 113

Walking the Florida Keys 118
Dagny Johnson Key Largo Hammock Botanical State Park
   31 Hammock Walk 120
John Pennekamp Coral Reef State Park
   32 Mangrove and Wild Tamarind Trails................................... 124
Windley Key Fossil Reef Geological State Park
   33 Sunset and Hammock Trails 129
Lignumvitae Key Botanical State Park
   34 Nature Trail 133
Long Key State Park
   35 Golden Orb and Layton Trails 137
Curry Hammock State Park
   36 Nature Trail 142
Marathon Bridge Walk
   37 Old Seven Mile Bridge to Pigeon Key 147
Bahia Honda State Park
   38 Silver Palm and Old Bridge Trails....................................... 150
National Key Deer Refuge
   39 Blue Hole and Nature Trails 155

Hiker's Checklist... 160
Index... 161
About the Author 163

Acknowledgments

A guidebook to Florida hiking is possible only because of the untiring efforts of the Florida Trail Association, the volunteer organization responsible for creating and maintaining many of the state's best wilderness hiking trails, including the Florida National Scenic Trail (also known as the Florida Trail and FNST).

Also responsible for opening up and conserving hundreds of miles of Florida pathways are the staffs and volunteer helpers of the Florida Park Service, the state and national forests, and the state and national wildlife refuges and preserves.

These are the people who have made it all possible for the rest of us.

Preface

No mountain high enough, no valley low enough…
what Florida hiking is like

The thirty-nine locations described here were selected to show the variety of Florida hiking, with walks ranging from under an hour to several days or even week-long backpacking trips. Yes, it's quite possible to lose yourself in the wilderness (even in heavily populated South Florida) for extended treks. Almost all of the thirty-nine highlighted locations have multiple trails and are true walking experiences not shared with cyclists, skateboarders and, in most places, horses, whose residual presence is never appreciated in our hot Florida climate.

Indeed, walks in South Florida can be as brief, or as long, as you wish. Although the majority are short nature walks of only an hour or two, you can always tackle the much longer treks that make up the 1,400-mile-long Florida Trail, one of eight National Scenic Trails; many of the segments are described here. Or, in the Keys, you can tackle over 200 miles of man-made paths from Key Largo to Key West in the southernmost region of the United States.

The hikes in South Florida are grouped according to their length in order to make it convenient to identify a walk that suits your particular requirements. They are divided into: Short Family Walks, Day and Overnight Hikes, and Long Haulers.

The trails of the Florida Keys, running from Key Largo down to Big Pine Key, are separated from the South Florida hikes. As you would expect, all of the Keys walks are quite short, unless you decide to see the Keys completely on its multiple-use Florida Keys Overseas Heritage Trail running almost the entire length of the islands (see the sidebar in Hike 36). Winter is the only sane time to attempt that.

Topographically, hiking South Florida and the Keys may be the easiest in all of North America. Florida, essentially a spit of sand between the Gulf of Mexico and the Atlantic Ocean, is an incredibly flat place. That puts almost all Florida hiking within the capabilities of anyone, from the youngest walker to the oldest. During the driest months—January to May—when the ground is hard, many of these trails are barrier free. Boardwalk nature trails at many of the state parks are well suited for wheelchairs year-round.

One point about Florida hiking that may trouble some out-of-state visitors: Your dog is not welcome on all trails, especially in South Florida. This is mostly for your pet's safety. South Florida is home to thousands of alligators, and alligators consider dogs among their favorite fast foods. If you plan to travel with your pet, check the Canine compatibility details with each hike.

"Walking is virtue, tourism deadly sin."
—Werner Herzog, film director

Introduction

What You'll See

The Florida peninsula is believed to be the last part of the continental United States to rise from the ocean, making it the youngest region geologically. Only Alaska can claim a longer shoreline.

South Florida and the Keys are classified as a subtropical region, receiving between 53 and 65 inches of rain a year. Relatively flat with a few rolling hills, South Florida and the Keys may not have the eye-popping panoramas of Colorado or Utah, but its landscape is quite striking in subtler ways.

The topography of South Florida and the Keys is usually classified according to its dominant biological communities, typically broken down as follows.

Biological Communities

Cypress swamp: The tall, gnarly bald cypress tree festooned with gray Spanish moss is the classic image of South Florida. Bald cypress swamps are usually found near rivers. The pond cypress, a second species, creates the cypress domes that occur on the prairies and in pine flatwood forests.

Only aquatic animals such as snakes, otters, and lizards can survive in cypress swamps flooded most of the year. Deer and wild hogs live in swamps inundated only seasonally. Wet or dry, cypress swamps also house a variety of other plants, such as ferns, bromeliads (air plants), saw grass, and pickerel weed.

Scrub cypress swamps: Most common to South Florida, scrub cypress swamps are much smaller than the above. Because vegetation is scant, animal life is correspondingly sparse. Alligators, deer, and wood storks are among the few residents.

Forest swamps: Also known as floodplain forest, these swamps are wet only part of the year. They are dominated by hardwoods such as water oak, black gum, sweet gum, and water hickory, with bald cypress and cabbage palm usually mixed in. Floodplain animals include bobcats, turkeys, deer, squirrels, otters, snakes, ducks, and songbirds.

Hammocks: In Florida the term "hammock" applies to any significant grouping of broad-leaved trees. A prime example is the live oak/cabbage palm hammocks of South Florida. The name comes from the Indian word meaning "shady place." All hammocks generally enjoy fertile soil, and the trees remain green year-round. Common animals are toads, flying squirrels, wood rats, and birds such as the flycatcher.

Salt marshes: Most commonly found along the coasts, salt marshes can be mixed in with mangroves or exist as a separate community. Black rush and cordgrass are the dominant plants. When salt marshes extend into tidal rivers, they often merge with freshwater marshes to form a fertile transition zone. Saltwater marshes are typically rich in bird and animal life, including otters, raccoons, turtles, and snakes.

Freshwater marshes: A blend of sedge, grass, and rush, freshwater marshes have standing water for two or more months out of the year. Land with a shorter period of standing water is classified as wet prairie. Freshwater marshes often house many endangered species. Look for wood storks, sandhill cranes, and Everglades kites. Alligators, wading birds and other waterfowl, frogs, turtles, and otters also thrive here.

Dry prairies: These treeless plains contain grasses and saw palmetto, with live oak/cabbage palm hammocks and dome cypress occasionally punctuating the flat spaces. A dry prairie may seem a lifeless, barren place, but closer inspection may reveal a considerable number of animals. Look for burrowing owls, sandhill cranes, raccoons, and bobcats.

Pine flatwoods: Pine flatwoods are the most common type of biological community in Florida, with three types of pine forests: Pond pines grow in wet conditions: longleaf pines in the higher and drier regions, and slash pines in the transition zone between the two. Although each forest type is dominated by its particular pine species, animal life is more diverse, including black bears, deer, bobcats, raccoons, gray foxes, squirrels, birds, and black snakes.

Sandhill areas: Fire is common in these dry and sparsely populated regions due to the arid conditions. It sometimes eliminates the longleaf pines, which are then supplanted by turkey and red oaks. Animals that burrow to avoid heat—and to escape the frequent fires—are common here: Gopher tortoises, indigo snakes, and pocket gophers are characteristic. In old-growth forest communities, you may be fortunate enough to spot the endangered red-cockaded woodpecker.

A burrowing owl stands beside its burrow.

Archaeology and History

Little is known about Florida's first native inhabitants, who date back 10,000 to 12,000 years. However, it's believed that about 2,000 years ago the population began to group itself according to geographical environment. This resulted in three distinctive Indian groups: in the subtropical Everglades, the central/north Florida St. Johns River Basin, and the Panhandle's northwest Gulf Coast.

Unfortunately, artifacts from this long period of habitation are sparse due to Florida's acidic soil. Nearly all that remains are stone tools—knives, arrowheads, and scrapers—including some from the earliest periods.

Hiking trails may cross sites of old Indian villages, and it's not unusual to find stone artifacts lying on the ground. Under the law, you're not allowed to dig anywhere, especially in the big humps of dirt or shells known as mounds, but anything you find on the surface is yours to keep. The best time to find stone arrowheads and knives is immediately after a good rain, which can wash away the top layer of soil to reveal either the whole artifact or edges of it sticking up through the dirt.

The Everglades

The Everglades is the largest remaining subtropical wilderness in the continental United States. Thanks to the popularity of Everglades National Park, many people believe the park is *the* Everglades. Unfortunately, it is not. Everglades National Park (1.5 million acres) and the adjoining Big Cypress National Preserve (716,000 acres) protect only about 20 percent of the huge area the Indians called Pahayokee, or "grassy waters."

In Everglades National Park, over 350 different species of birds have been sighted, of which about 200 are migratory that visit primarily during the winter months. Sixteen types of wading birds live in the park year-round; the wood stork is the largest.

Over a million people a year visit Everglades National Park just south of Miami near Homestead to see the profusion of bird and animal life that is America's equivalent of an African big game safari. Many animals are so accustomed to seeing three-eyed humans (that third eye being a camera lens), you'll be able to approach them quite closely.

What Makes the Everglades Unique?

The terrain of the Everglades is extremely low and flat, with the highest point only about 8 feet above water. Obviously, the terrain hasn't risen very far since it was part of the sea bottom as recently as 6,000 to 8,000 years ago.

The bedrock beneath the Glades is unusual. Known as *oolite* or "egg stone," oolite granules resemble a cluster of fish eggs. This is the result of South Florida repeatedly sinking into the sea and then re-emerging from it, which has occurred at least four times in recent geologic history. Each time the land disappeared, millions of plants and animals perished, decomposed, and deposited calcium carbonate on the sea floor. In turn, the calcium carbonate hardened around grains of sand to create the oolite.

A visit to the Everglades is almost like a visit to the Caribbean: Everglades plants are more akin to those of the Caribbean than North America. The gumbo limbo with its reddish bark and twisting branches is one of the best-known examples.

Although tree hammocks are found throughout the park, the Everglades primarily are a shallow plain of saw grass growing in water only 6 inches deep. This blanket of water has been likened to a tropical, primordial soup of algae and bacteria. Unappetizing as that may sound, it nourishes snakes, turtles, fish, and insects, which in turn feed the incredibly rich population of birds.

Traditionally the Glades' most important water source has been Lake Okeechobee, located 60 miles north of the park. Each summer, Lake Okeechobee (the second-largest freshwater lake in the continental United States) would overflow and send a sheet of water 50 miles wide that moved over the landscape. The water advanced about 100 feet a day, thoroughly watering and flushing the saw grass, eventually reaching the mangrove estuaries on the Gulf of Mexico.

This annual flood was always followed by a six-month dry season. Birds and animals adapted and patterned their lives based on this alternating cycle.

The Human Impact

Archaeologists say that at least three different Indian tribes lived in the Everglades before Europeans arrived. Indians living in the western-most region were called Caloosa; those around Lake Okeechobee in the central section were the Mayaimi; the Indians living near the east coast were the Tequesta. The names of these two latter tribes are memorialized in the names of two South Florida cities, Miami and Tequesta.

Small Miccosukee Indian villages like this one are a common sight on the Tamiami Trail connecting Miami and Naples.

Most of the Native Americans you see in the Everglades today are descendants of the Seminoles who moved into the area in the late 1700s and early 1800s. They remained free here only because the land was considered so inhospitable that no one else wanted it.

However, Everglades soil was found to be rich and fertile, so beginning in the twentieth century, massive attempts were made to regulate the water flow for the benefit of farmers and cattlemen. From 1905 to 1925, the state and federal governments opened several thousand acres for farming, but a hurricane in 1928 caused considerable destruction and killed 1,800 people. That prompted the federal government to dam and dike Lake Okeechobee to prevent another such disaster.

A disaster occurred anyway. This time, it was the wildlife that suffered. Though the Everglades may receive 60 or more inches of rain in a year, almost four-fifths of it is lost to evaporation and runoff. Consequently, Lake Okeechobee's floodwaters have always been essential to maintain the proper, delicate balance. By altering Okeechobee's annual overflow, life in the Glades was severely disrupted once the wetlands was cut to a small fraction of its original size.

The statistics are almost sickening. Today, between 50,000 and 100,000 wading birds inhabit in the park, dramatically fewer than the estimated 255,000 residing here in the 1930s.

For a time, the once-thriving alligator population also plummeted. Gators, like the water birds, suffered not because there was too little water—instead, there was often far too much of it. Gators build their nests at the normal high-water level, and if floodgates release more water and the level goes higher, the gator nests are flooded and destroyed.

Another species virtually decimated was the snail kite. The entire North American population declined to an estimated two dozen birds by the 1960s. Snail kites feed predominantly on apple snails, which lay their eggs above the high-water line. Add too much water, and there go the snails. Wood storks, considered one of the key barometers of the Everglades' health, were classified as endangered in the 1980s due to their rapid decline.

Everglades' water quality also seriously deteriorated due to massive runoffs of farm nutrients that kill beneficial algae and promote the growth of harmful marsh vegetation. The dairy industry was one of the most unlikely culprits: A single dairy cow daily produces as much raw waste as twenty people, and there are a lot of dairy cattle in the water basin that supports the Everglades.

High levels of mercury, evidently fallout from power plants and other sources, have also infected the food chain. In fact, fishermen today are advised to limit their consumption of freshwater fish from the Everglades to about one a week.

On top of all this, people are in the process of drinking Florida dry. Florida has the fourth-largest population in the United States and it is still growing. An estimated 1,000 persons move into the Sunshine State each and every day, a group that gulps down or flushes another 200,000 gallons of water daily. Another forty million visitors drink and flush water on their vacations.

To accommodate the state's rapid growth, Florida officials have been busy paving over the land to build roads, homes, schools, and shopping centers, which has reduced the amount of rainwater reaching the underground aquifers that supply the water in the first place.

If the water table continues to drop, saltwater incursion into the freshwater aquifer could have dire consequences. Not only would it impact soil quality and the ability of plants to grow, it would eliminate the potable water. People would have to rely on desalinization plants, quite a costly process.

As you will discover on any of its hiking trails, the Everglades is an irreplaceable land that can provide many unforgettable experiences. Shouldn't your descendants enjoy them, too? Anytime you hear Congress or anyone else discussing the fate and future of the Everglades, let your elected representatives know how important this region is to you.

We all need to be vigilant about keeping the Everglades a memorable place—and not let it fade into a memory.

What to Avoid Outdoors

Heat and humidity: These are the two biggest drawbacks of hiking in South Florida and the Keys. From June until as late as mid-November, the temperatures routinely soar into the 90-degree range, sometimes over 100 degrees, making it too hot to hike comfortably except during early morning.

How comfortable you are depends on the combined effects of humidity and air temperature. The National Oceanic and Atmospheric Association (NOAA) offers the following chart as a guideline.

Air Temperature	Percent Humidity									
	10%	20%	30%	40%	50%	60%	70%	80%	90%	100%
	Feels Like									
125°F	123	141								
120°F	116	130	148							
115°F	111	120	135	151						
110°F	105	112	123	137	150					
105°F	100	105	113	123	135	149				
100°F	95	99	104	110	120	132	144			
95°F	90	93	96	101	107	114	124	136		
90°F	85	87	90	93	96	100	106	113	122	
85°F	80	82	84	86	88	90	93	97	102	108
80°F	75	77	78	79	81	82	85	86	88	91
75°F	70	72	73	74	75	76	77	78	79	80
70°F	65	66	67	68	69	70	70	71	71	72

Summer humidity often falls into the 60 to 80 percent range, which is why South Floridians usually limit their daytime summer activity to moving from one air-conditioned spot to the next. Locals like to label anyone over the age of twenty-five with a summer tan as a tourist or a recent transplant.

Mosquitoes: Saltwater mosquitoes are active year-round in coastal areas while freshwater mosquitoes are mostly limited to the summer/fall rainy season. Wearing a long-sleeved shirt and long pants and applying insect repellent is the best defense. Mosquitoes typically become most active around twilight, a good time to be off the trail, hiding in a tent, or standing around a smoky fire.

West Nile Virus: In Florida, more people are killed by lightning annually than by the West Nile virus. The Centers for Disease Control and Prevention (CDC) advises that the best protection against mosquitoes and other biting insects is an insect repellent containing DEET. In addition, spray your clothing with repellents containing permethrin or another Environmental Protection Agency (EPA)–registered repellent, since mosquitoes may bite through thin clothing. Do not apply repellents containing permethrin directly to exposed skin or to skin under your clothing. For the latest information on the West Nile virus, visit www.cdc.gov/ncidod/dvbid/westnile.

Lightning: Frequent thunderstorm activity ranks Florida as one of the world's lightning capitals. In South Florida and the Keys you're more likely to be zapped by lightning than fatally bitten by a rattlesnake (which are at their liveliest in summer). July and August are peak lightning months, but there are lots of thunderstorms in June and September.

When a thunderstorm approaches:

- Stay away from the beach or any type of water.
- Try to get through the storm in a low spot under a thick stand of small trees.
- Avoid tall trees in open fields, trees at the water's edge, or trees whose roots are in damp soil.
- Don't shelter under oaks or pine trees. Because of their high starch content, they are among the best natural conductors of electricity.
- If you're wearing an aluminum-frame backpack, take it off—and stay well away from it until the storm passes.
- Stay away from wire fences or any pieces of metal that could conduct lightning to you.
- A tingling sensation in your scalp is a warning that a bolt may be about to strike: Fall to the ground immediately.

Hurricanes: Called "hurrican, the evil spirit" by the Indians, these storms can affect hiking conditions. Hurricane season begins in June, with the greatest activity typically in August, September, and October. As the saying about Florida's hurricane season goes: "June too soon, July stand by, August and September remember, October all over."

Hunting season: Hiking is forbidden in some areas during the first week of the hunting season starting in November and also the period between Christmas and the New Year, when hunting is at its peak. The rest of the hunting season, hikers must wear a fluorescent orange vest (available at sporting goods stores). Never wear anything white—the white-tailed deer is the favorite target. Weekdays normally see the fewest hunters in the woods. Trails located in hunting areas are identified in the description section. There is no hunting in the Keys.

Dehydration: By far, this is the greatest danger you'll probably face when hiking in Florida. Thirst, dry lips, and a parched throat all are signs of dehydration. Here's how you can maintain your energy:

- **Consume liquids** even when you're not thirsty.
- **Maintain the proper potassium level** (take supplements from health food stores, drink tea, or eat bananas).
- **Avoid colas and alcohol.** They are diuretics that could dehydrate you even more.
- **Take advantage of air-conditioning.** You will probably feel more rested if you sleep in an air-conditioned room following any extended hike.

Prickly heat: In constant humidity, it's easy to develop a rash. Avoid rashes by powdering yourself in the morning and evening with talcum powder or powder containing zinc. Also wear loose-fitting pants and comfortable shirts made of lightweight cotton.

Sunburn: Florida's sun is far more intense than anywhere else in the continental United States except for extreme elevations. Gradual exposure to the sun is essential. So is wearing a water-resistant sunblock (SPF 25 to 30). The best protection is to cover your skin by wearing a long-sleeved shirt, long pants, and a broad-brimmed hat.

Untreated Water: In general, no water along Florida trails is safe to drink. Don't let clarity fool you: If you use spring or river water for cooking, boil it about five minutes to kill all parasites. Or use a filter designed to remove all parasites, including Giardia. Never drink salt water, no matter how thirsty you are.

Intestinal problems: Such afflictions are usually the result of a bacterial infection or from consuming strange food and drink. Always carry your own water, and avoid drinking from streams, no matter how clear/clean they look.

Poisonous plants: Poison ivy and poison sumac can be a problem. Touching either can produce a skin irritation that may develop small, itchy blisters. Poison ivy is a shrub that may be found growing upright or on the ground; it is characterized by leaves comprising three leaflets and berries that are often whitish. Poison sumac is a bush with leaves comprising seven to thirteen leaflets and white berries. Cortisone cream is an effective remedy for both.

Getting lost: Most hiking trails in South Florida and the Keys are clearly blazed, so getting lost may require some concerted effort. Always carry a map, a compass, and a whistle (three blasts is the universal call for assistance), plus a flashlight in case you don't make it back before dark. And take your cell phone.

The Rogues' Gallery: Animals and Insects

Rabid raccoons: This designation isn't meant to be humorous but to drive home the point that sometimes rabies is a problem in South Florida and the Keys. Animals that are overly friendly or aggressive and that seem to have no fear of humans are definitely suspect.

Chiggers: These small red mites are fond of attacking around the ankles, waist, and wrists, where they burrow under the skin and cause severe itching. Putting clear nail polish on the chigger bites will often smother any critters still in the skin. Calamine lotion helps relieve the itching.

Fire ants: Fire ant mounds are readily spotted—they look like shovelfuls of dirt. The danger is accidentally stepping on a mound and having the ants swarm up your legs. As many as half a million fire ants live in a colony. Anyone allergic to ant bites should carry appropriate medication, just in case.

Ticks: Because of region's warm climate, ticks are active almost year-round. Because of the danger of Lyme disease, it is essential to always use repellent in the woods and to check your clothing and body for ticks after a hike is over. When camping, spray your tent and sleeping bag with repellent. LYMErix, a vaccine against Lyme disease, is estimated to be about 80 percent effective.

No-see-ums: For the most part, only beach hikers at sunrise and sunset need to worry about no-see-ums, midges or sand flies so tiny they are almost invisible. Long pants and shoes and socks are the best protection.

Spiders: Although wolf spiders and jumping spiders can inflict painful wounds, only two species of spiders are a serious threat to humans: the black widow and brown recluse. Black widows can be found in woodpiles, inside stone and wood walls, in outdoor toilets, and anywhere else that offers a good hiding place. A black widow bite requires an immediate visit to the hospital for antivenin, since about 5 percent of all black widow bites are fatal. The brown recluse spider—also known as the fiddleback or violin spider because of the distinctive violin-shaped marking on its back—is not deadly, but the venom from its bite actually causes body tissue around the inflicted area to disintegrate. Without medical treatment, the wound will continue to deepen and may take months to heal.

Snakes: Florida has a larger snake population than any other state, but snakes are rarely a problem if you stick to the trails, don't haphazardly step over logs without looking, and exercise common sense. Six Florida snake species are poisonous, and half of those are rattlesnakes: eastern diamondback rattlesnake, canebrake rattlesnake and pygmy rattlesnake. Others include the cottonmouth water moccasin, coral snake, and copperhead (found mostly in the Panhandle).

The coral snake is related to mambas and cobras and is said to be the country's most poisonous snake. Fortunately, it is rarely a problem, since it must almost gnaw on a person to break the skin. Most bites occur when people pick up "the pretty snake" to examine it. Coral snakes make their homes in brush piles, rotting logs, and pinewoods. The coral is sometimes confused with the harmless king snake, which also has colorful markings. The way to tell the two apart: "Red touch yellow, kill a fellow; red touch black, won't hurt Jack." Not great poetry, but it makes its point.

If someone is bitten, the best treatment may be to do nothing except take the person immediately to a hospital. Cutting the skin and attempting to suck out the venom often does considerable harm, sometimes severing muscle tissue.

Alligators: This is last on the list of hazards, and for good reason. Unless you swim in a remote lake during the spring mating season, when alligators sometimes go a little crazy, or during low water levels, when they have been known to attack swimmers and even a lakeside jogger, gators should not pose a danger. Alligators normally run or disappear when they encounter a human unless they have been fed by people or you are accompanied by a dog (a favorite alligator snack). Never harass an alligator or get between the animal and its body of water.

Florida Trail Association

The first blaze for the Florida National Scenic Trail (FNST), or Florida Trail, was painted on a tree in the Ocala National Forest. It was the dream of a brand-new organization called the Florida Trail Association (FTA) to blaze a walkway running north-south through the entire state. They succeeded so well that in 1983 the Florida Trail was designated one of only eight National Scenic Trails by the U.S. Congress.

The FTA is a group of dedicated hikers who still work hard maintaining the FNST. With eighteen chapters and almost 5,000 members, each year the FTA sends hundreds of volunteers to the woods to clear the way and preserve the vital system of tree blazes that lead hikers safely through the densest forest. About three-fourths of the 1,400-mile-long trail now consists of natural corridor. At completion, the FNST is expected to contain 1,800 miles of hiking trails. An estimated 1.8 million people walk some section of the trail each year.

Trail Blazes

Most of the blazes on Florida trails have been placed there by the FTA. The eye-level blazes are normally quite easy to spot. This is the FTA system:

- **Orange blazes** mark the main trail.
- **Blue blazes** designate side trails to developed campgrounds or a natural site of unusual interest. In some state forests, blue blazes mark the equestrian trail.
- **White blazes** mark the trails in many state parks.
- **A double blaze** signals a change in direction. It could also mean the trail is no longer taking the most obvious route. Don't leave a double blaze until you've spotted the next single blaze.

The FTA sponsors approximately 500 different activities that take place throughout the state each year. Members are kept informed through a bimonthly newsletter.

For information about joining, contact the Florida Trail Association, 5413 Southwest Thirteenth Street, Gainesville, FL 32608; (877) HIKE-FLA; e-mail: fta@florida trail.org; or visit www.floridatrail.org.

Florida State Parks

Perhaps the most underrated and underappreciated segment of the Florida outdoors is that managed by the state park system, which oversees the majority of the best day hikes and many outstanding natural areas. Florida State Parks manages almost 160 locations and adds new ones regularly as more land is purchased and put under protection. About fourteen million people visit the state parks annually.

In 2005, for the second time in five years, Florida State Parks received the National Gold Medal Award for excellence in Recreation Management from the National Recreation and Park Association. This was the first time a state park system anywhere has received the recognition twice.

Camping in State Parks

About 50 of Florida's 160 state parks offer camping, with a total of more than 3,300 campsites. Reservations can be made up to eleven months in advance by calling (800) 326-3521 between 8:00 a.m. and 8:00 p.m. or visiting www.reserveamerica .com. Although the parks stay open until sunset year-round, you should check in between 8:00 a.m. and 5:00 p.m. Fees range from $12 to $28 according to park

Wildlife has the right-of-way in all South Florida parks and preserves.

location, season, and whether you use water and electricity. Not all state parks accept pets in campgrounds. For parks that do allow pets, check out www.floridastateparks.org/campcabinlodge.cfm. Look under "Pet Camping."

State Park Annual Passes

If you're going to spend considerable time in state parks in South Florida and the Keys, you'll probably want to investigate the annual entrance passes for individuals and for families of up to eight people. They are available online (www.floridastateparks .org/annualpass), at the parks, or by calling (352) 628-7002. The cost is $43.40 for an individual, $85.80 for families. Camping fees are extra. For information about Florida State Parks, including entrance fee schedules, call (850) 245-2157 or visit www.floridastateparks.org.

Hiking Techniques

Treading Lightly

Florida's warm weather and unique landscape are the main reasons so many people move to the Sunshine State. South Florida and the Keys are in danger of being loved to death. As more and more land is developed into sites for homes, schools, and shopping malls, the forests and preserves become ever more precious. Although South Florida and the Keys may become ever more crowded, large sections of wilderness land must endure.

Here's how you can help:

- Always stay on the designated trails.
- Leave wildflowers, air plants, and other foliage where you find them.
- Never walk on sand dunes.
- Camp only in designated areas.
- Be especially careful of campfires.
- Be careful of human waste. Bury it at least 6 inches deep, a minimum of 200 feet from any water and 100 feet from any campsite.
- Wash dishes at least 200 feet from streams and lakes.
- Don't leave unwanted souvenirs. Pack out everything.

Hiking with Children

In planning any outing with children, remember with whom you are hiking. Don't be surprised or upset when they act like kids. Five- and six-year-olds are often capable of hiking for short distances, but they are not apt to be prepared for all-day trips. A walk of an hour or two is a good way to introduce children to the outdoors.

Short nature walks like those listed in Short Family Walks will have far more appeal than a simple two-hour jaunt through the woods where the fairly undramatic scenery doesn't change much. Interesting nature walks are the easiest way to create a life-long interest in the outdoors and all its diversity.

Encourage older children to carry their own packs. Some kids will want to bring favorite toys or books along. Children learn from their parents by example. Hiking and camping trips are excellent opportunities to teach young ones to tread lightly and minimize their imprint upon the environment.

How to Use This Guide

This book does not attempt to cover every trail or walking path in South Florida and the Keys. Instead, it is limited to thirty-nine of the best locations offering the most varied hikes—often multiple walks as described in detail here—that offer the chance to observe unspoiled, natural Florida at its finest. The maps are based on topographic maps issued by state of Florida agencies and the National Park Service, and we used the *DeLorme Florida Atlas & Gazetter* as an additional resource.

Unless you are making an extended hike on a long section of the Florida National Scenic Trail, you should find these maps adequate. For long-range hikes you may want to purchase a map from the Forest Service or the Florida Trail Association. Each trail is evaluated according to difficulty, but that is often based more on the length of the hike than the terrain conditions, which are normally quite flat.

However, these estimates may not take into account wet or muddy conditions resulting from prolonged rain or other natural events. These appraisals are only guidelines, subject to changing conditions, and should not be taken as unchanging gospel. Any time the weather has been unusually wet or dry, consult with the appropriate on-site agency listed with every trail. In summer and early fall, some trails routinely flood after heavy rains.

The distances provided should be taken only as guidelines, not precise absolutes. Although I sometimes walked with as many as three pedometers, it was rare that all three instruments agreed at every point of a hike.

Trail Finder Chart

Trail Finder Chart ★ The Homestead area of Everglades National Park offers all of these facilities except cabins/lodging, but they may be far removed from the various trailheads.

Number	Hike	Fishing	Cabins	Primitive Camping	Camp-ground	Swimming	Canoeing/ Kayaking	Bicycling	Beach	Wildlife/ Nature
1	Myakka River State Park	●		●		●	●	●		●
2	Highlands Hammock State Park	●				●	●	●	●	●
3	Six Mile Cypress Slough Preserve	●				●	●		●	●
4	Corkscrew Swamp Sanctuary	●			●	●	●		●	●
5	Florida Panther NWR	●				●	●	●		●
6	Fakahatchee Strand Preserve State Park	●		●				●		●
★7	Everglades: Anhinga Trail	●	●	●		●	●	●		●
★8	Everglades: Gumbo Limbo Trail		●	●	●	●	●			●
★9	Everglades: Pinelands Short Loop									●
★10	Everglades: Pa–Hay–Okee Overlook Trail	●		●		●	●	●		●
★11	Everglades: Mahogany Hammock Trail		●		●		●			●
★12	Everglades: West Lake Mangrove Trail	●					●			●
★13	Everglades: Eco Pond Trail			●			●			●

Number	Hike	Fishing	Cabins	Primitive Camping	Camp-ground	Swimming	Canoeing/ Kayaking	Bicycling	Beach	Wildlife/ Nature
*14	Everglades: Bayshore Loop Trail									●
*15	Everglades: Shark Valley									●
16	Loxahatchee NWR	●		●				●		●
17	J.W. Corbett WMA: Hungryland									●
18	Oscar Scherer State Park: Yellow Trail	●		●	●	●	●	●		●
19	Oscar Scherer State Park: Blue Trail				●	●	●			●
20	Oscar Scherer State Park: Red Trail	●	●	●	●	●	●			●
21	Oscar Scherer State Park: Green Trail			●				●		●
22	Ding Darling NWR: Indigo Trail	●		●	●	●	●	●		●
23	Ding Darling NWR: Shell Mound Trail			●						●
24	Ding Darling NWR: Bailey Tract	●			●		●			●
25	Everglades: Pinelands Long Loop	●		●	●		●	●		●

Trail Finder

Number	Hike	Fishing	Cabins	Primitive Camping	Camp-ground	Swimming	Canoeing/ Kayaking	Bicycling	Beach	Wildlife/ Nature
26	Everglades: Snake Bight/Rowdy Bend Trails	•			•	•	•	•		•
27	Everglades: Bear Lake Trail									•
28	Jonathan Dickinson SP									•
29	J.W. Corbett WMA: Florida Trail Segment									•
30	DuPuis Management Area									•
31	Dagny Johnson Key Largo Hammock Botanical SP							•		•
32	John Pennekamp Coral Reef SP									•
33	Windley Key Fossil Reef Geological SP									•
34	Lignumvitae Key Botanical SP									•
35	Long Key SP									•
36	Curry Hammock SP									•
37	Marathon Bridge Walk									•
38	Bahia Honda SP									•
39	National Key Deer Refuge									•

Map Legend

Transportation

Interstate Highway	═══⬭15⬭═══
U.S. Highway	═══⬭27⬭═══
State Road	═══⬭19⬭═══
County Road	═══[CR27]═══
Forest Road	═══[FR314]═══
Dirt Road	═ ═ ═ ═ ═
Railroad	├─┼─┼─┼─┤
Featured Trail	▬ ▬ ▬ ▬ ▬
Other Trail	‐ ‐ ‐ ‐ ‐ ‐

Hydrology

Lake/Reservoir	
River/Creek	
Marsh/Swamp	
Mangrove Swamps	
Well	●

Land Use

State Park/State Forest	

Symbols

Campground	⛺
Point of Interest	■
Visitor Center	?
Parking	P
Picnic Area	⛱
Ranger Station	🏛
Tower	♖
City/Town	○
Trailhead (Start)	❺
Bridge	≍
Gate	•━•
Bench	▬

Scale

0	Kilometer	1
0	Mile	1

True North
(Magnetic North is
approximately 15.5° East) N ⬥

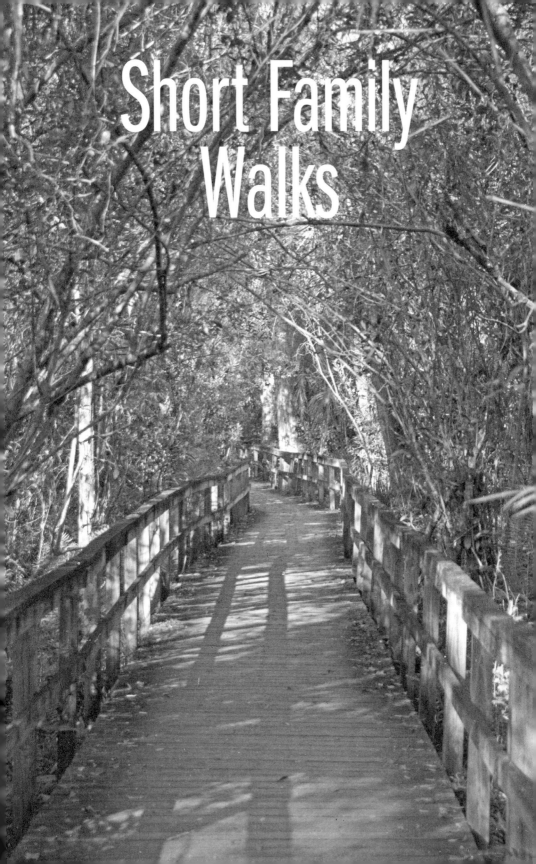

Short Family Walks

1 Myakka River State Park: Canopy Walkway and Boylston Nature Trail

The canopy walk in Myakka River State Park is one of only two in the entire United States and the only one in a subtropical forest.

This popular park near Sarasota features North America's first canopy walkway located in a subtropical forest. Canopy walkways have a sound scientific value, offering a way to study forest treetops that otherwise would be difficult to reach. Forests have been compared to giant stands of lollipops with all the sugar production taking place high overhead. And the birds, insects, and other animals that depend on them also spend much of their time well away from the ground.

On the 85-foot-long Myakka Canopy Walkway, you're perched 25 feet off the ground, suspended between two towers with winding stairways. One of the towers is 35 feet high. The other, 74 feet tall, offers an excellent view of the forest canopy.

Shortly after this canopy walk opened, scientists using it discovered the local presence of a Central American weevil that arrived in Fort Lauderdale in 1990. This was the first indication the beetle had moved into Southwest Florida. Studies are being conducted here that may help stop the weevil, which destroys air plants.

The Canopy Trail is a short spur on the William S. Boylston Nature Trail, which explores a mix of open prairies, wetlands, and hardwood hammock. Both trails may be underwater during summer and fall due to rain. Check ahead.

The Fakahatchee Strand boardwalk penetrates the Big Cypress Swamp.

Nearest town: Sarasota
Start: Boylston Nature Trail parking lot
Distance: 0.8 mile lollipop loop
Approximate hiking time: 45 to 60 minutes
Difficulty: Easy
Trail surface: Primarily natural surface
Seasons: Late fall through early spring
Other trail users: Hikers only
Canine compatibility: No pets above ground on the canopy walkway, in concession areas, cabins, or restrooms. Where allowed, pets must be on 6-foot leash and not unattended.
Land status: State park
Fees and permits: Park admission under $5
Schedule: Open daily, 8:00 a.m. to sunset
Maps: Available at park office
Trail contact: Myakka River State Park, 13207 State Road 72, Sarasota, FL 34241-9542; (941) 361-6511; www.floridastateparks.org/myakkariver
Special consideration: When the Myakka River floods, so do the trails.

Finding the trailhead: Myakka River State Park is located east of Sarasota on State Road 72 (Clark Road), 9 miles east of Interstate 75 (exit 205). The park entrance is on the left (north). The nature trail and walkway are located on the right immediately after crossing the bridge over the Myakka River. **GPS:** N27 14.785' W08218.162'

The Hike

This park is excellent for weekend family outings. The marked Boylston Nature Trail begins at the parking lot on the right just beyond the bridge over the Myakka River. It is also the trailhead to the Canopy Walkway. You start by walking through a low area of cabbage palms and saw palmetto, almost immediately coming to the spur trail leading off to the right and the canopy walk.

Building the walkway was a major undertaking, requiring 2,571 hours to build, 47 percent of the work provided by volunteers. An information sign helps place in perspective the importance—and uniqueness—of this aerial platform. Currently, only thirty canopy walkways exist worldwide, eleven of them situated in Latin and South American rain and cloud forests. Peru boasts the world's longest walkway, measuring 0.25 mile long and strung 120 feet high over the Amazon jungle. The United States claims nine walkways—two in Florida but only one in a subtropical forest, at Myakka State Park.

▶ A guided nature walk is held year-round in Myakka River State Park on Saturday at 9:00 a.m.; (941) 361-6511. Safari tram tours of the park's backcountry are offered from mid-December through May.

Since the walkway basically is a swinging bridge hanging between two towers, do expect it to swing, though not badly. Look for birds, butterflies, and air plants as you climb the tower steps. From the top of the taller 74-foot tower, enjoy the excellent view of the bright green palm canopy surprisingly far below you.

Completing the walkway, retrace your steps to the junction with the Boylston Nature Trail; turn right at the junction. This nature trail features two long boardwalks

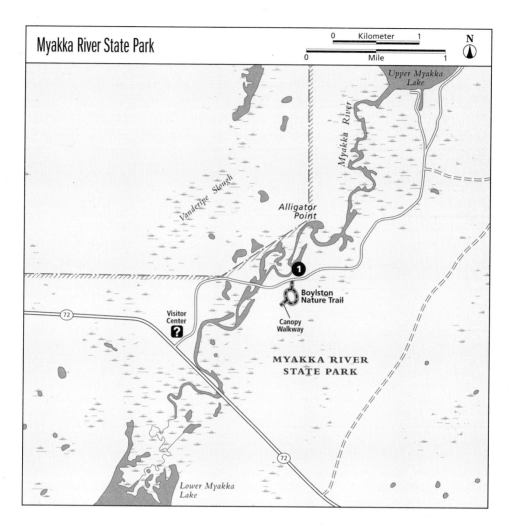

Myakka River State Park

crossing a low marsh that will probably be devoid of bird life if the water level is low. Dry ground may be the more comfortable condition for hiking, but it isn't usually well suited for wildlife viewing.

After going over the open marsh, you'll enter an area thick with saw palmettos. Note how the pathway bordering the palmettos is torn up with pig rooting. Descendents of the feral pigs introduced by the Spanish in the 1500s thrive throughout Florida in most wooded areas close to water. At first glance feral hogs may resemble domestic pigs, but the wild animals are leaner with a coarser, denser coat and a longer, narrower head. The males usually have razor-sharp tusks from 2 to 5 inches long. Females have smaller tusks.

Florida's wild hog population is now out of control, with an estimated half-million of the razorbacks knocking down and trampling large amounts of native vegetation as well as farm crops. Rooting, where the hogs dig for foods underground, causes the most damage since it uproots or weakens vegetation and helps cause erosion. This path with pig rooting literally everywhere is a prime example. By feeding on tree seeds and seedlings, the hogs cause such significant damage in forests they may make it more difficult to regenerate long-leaf pine forests. Since the hogs are so well established and such prolific breeders, there seems little chance of ever eliminating them.

Once you leave this torn-up area (which I call Hog Wallow) via the second boardwalk over a marsh, the trail starts looping out of the hammock and back toward the trailhead. This is a better area in which to see white-tailed deer.

Miles and Directions

0.0 Leave from the roadside parking area, a common trailhead for Boylston Nature Trail and Canopy Walkway. In about 200 feet, the trail Ts. Go right to the canopy walk.

0.1 Arrive at the canopy boardwalk. After climbing the walkway, retrace your steps to junction with Boylston Nature Trail.

0.2 At junction with Boylston Nature Trail, turn right to join nature walk.

0.3 Take boardwalk across marsh. Go straight.

0.4 Enter palmetto area and "hog wallow."

0.6 Take the second boardwalk back across the marsh.

0.7 Trail makes a sharp right.

0.8 Arrive back at the parking lot.

More Information

Local Information
Sarasota Convention and Visitors Bureau: www.sarasotafl.org.
Sarasota Chamber of Commerce: www.sarasotachamber.com.

Local Events/Attractions
For **backpackers,** Myakka River State Park includes a 36-mile section of the Florida National Scenic Trail (FNST) that also can be divided into shorter day segments. (For details, see *Hiking Florida: A Guide to Florida's Greatest Hiking Adventures,* The Globe Pequot Press.)

Canoe or kayak 14 miles of the Myakka Wild and Scenic River. Bring your own or rent one. There are several access points to the river within the park. During low water in winter and spring, some portaging may be required.

Rangers conduct **nature walks** on Saturday at 9:00 a.m. Half-hour **campfire programs** are held from Thanksgiving through Easter on Saturday at 7:30 p.m. During the same winter period, **Beginning Birding** is offered on Sunday at 9:00 a.m. Binoculars and field guides are provided.

Two large airboats make year-round **scenic cruises** several times daily on the Upper Myakka Lake, venturing into shallow regions off-limits to traditional crafts. Tram safaris explore the backcountry every afternoon from December 16 to May 31. For prices and times, visit www.floridastateparks.org/myakkariver/activities.cfm.

Lodging
Five historic log cabins in the park hold up to six people each; no pets are permitted.

Camping

There are 5 campsites in the park, the first a little more than 4 miles in. There are also 76 developed sites. Reservations can be made through Reserve America: (800) 326-3521; www.reserveamerica .com/index.jsp.

Organizations

Florida Department of Environmental Protection/Division of Recreation and Parks: www.dep .state.fl.us/parks.

The giant leather fern grows in canals and ditches in tropical swamps. Spores grow on the underside of the fronds, like rust-brown felt.

2 Highlands Hammock State Park: Nature Trails

The swamp areas of Highlands Hammock hold a healthy alligator population. Forget about taking a pet with you.

You'll feel truly humbled standing next to a 1,000-year-old oak tree on the Big Oak Trail, one of Highlands Hammock State Park's most popular nature trails. The old tree's gnarled and twisted girth is an incredible 37.5 feet; you'll never worry about being overweight again.

Huge, ancient oaks are only one of the many attractions at this 5,540-acre park. Local citizens, concerned about this hammock turning into farmland, purchased the property in the early 1930s to protect it. Considering the tremendous development close to the park these days, visitors will readily appreciate the foresight of these people as they walk any of the nine different nature trails that explore the virgin forest hammock. Many of the trails, which are amazingly diverse and specialized, are wheelchair accessible.

Nearest town: Sebring
Start: With one exception, all start from the main park road, Hammock Road
Distance: Just over 5 miles for all trails
Approximate hiking time: 3 to 4 hours; you don't just barrel through these trails
Difficulty: Easy
Trail surface: Boardwalk and natural path
Seasons: Fall through spring
Other trail users: Hikers only

Canine compatibility: Leashed pets can go anywhere except boardwalks.
Land status: State park
Fees and permits: Entrance fee under $5
Schedule: Open 8:00 a.m. until sunset daily
Maps: None needed; map on park brochure
Trail contact: Highlands Hammock State Park, 5931 Hammock Road, Sebring, FL 33872; (863) 386-6094; www.floridastateparks.org/ highlandshammock

Finding the trailhead: Take U.S. Highway 27 to Sebring and turn west onto County Road 634, just north of Sebring. Follow CR 634 about 3 miles to the park entrance. All but one of the trails begin off the main park road, Hammock Road, and are clearly signed.

Hickory–Big Oak–Wild Orange Grove Trails
GPS: N27 28.352' W081 32.565'

The Hike

Link three different trails together to create a longer hike totaling 2 miles, including retracing your steps. You could break this walk into shorter sections, but if you intend to hike all the trails, this is the most efficient way to avoid car shuttling.

▶ When Florida's state park system was finally established in 1935, Highlands Hammock was one of the first four original state parks.

Park at the Hickory Trail parking lot at the first pull off on the right on Hammock Road. Take the Hickory Trail to the Big Oak Trail, where you'll see that massive old oak split in the middle with a cavity large enough for a person to stand in. It's easy to believe this is the park's famous thousand-year-old tree, but it isn't. That tree is located a little farther on.

Continue to join the Big Oak Trail, going left where the path forms a T. Cross a long, narrow boardwalk that leads to the truly ancient oak, a gnarled and knotted creature that resembles one of the ancient Ents in the magical forests known to Hobbits and Orcs. With a circumference of 37.5 feet and an estimated age of 1,000 years, the tree is officially labeled a laurel oak, most of which don't normally last beyond 100 years. It's been theorized the tree may be a laurel oak/live oak cross.

Finishing the Big Oak Trail, cross the park road to start the Wild Orange Grove Trail, aptly named after the citrus trees planted in the 1800s by those who settled the area. Earlier in the walk you may have seen grapefruit trees, but the scattered fruit trees in this section are remnants of the orange orchard. This is a wetter area where wild hog rooting is common in the mixed forest that includes cabbage palms and laurel oaks. After going through a hardwood hammock, the path ends at the Hammock Inn, where you can sample such specialties as wild orange cream pie and ice cream. The Inn's hours and days vary by season; call ahead (863-385-7025). After a snack, it's time to retrace your steps.

Miles and Directions

0.0 Start from Hickory Trail parking lot on Hammock Road.

0.2 Trail Ts. Go left to join Big Oak Trail.

0.4 Cross Hammock Road to start Wild Orange Grove Trail.

0.6 Enter hardwood hammock.

1.0 Reach Hammock Inn. Retrace your steps.

2.0 Return to Hickory Trail parking lot. The Fern Garden trailhead is located directly across the street.

Highlands Hammock State Park

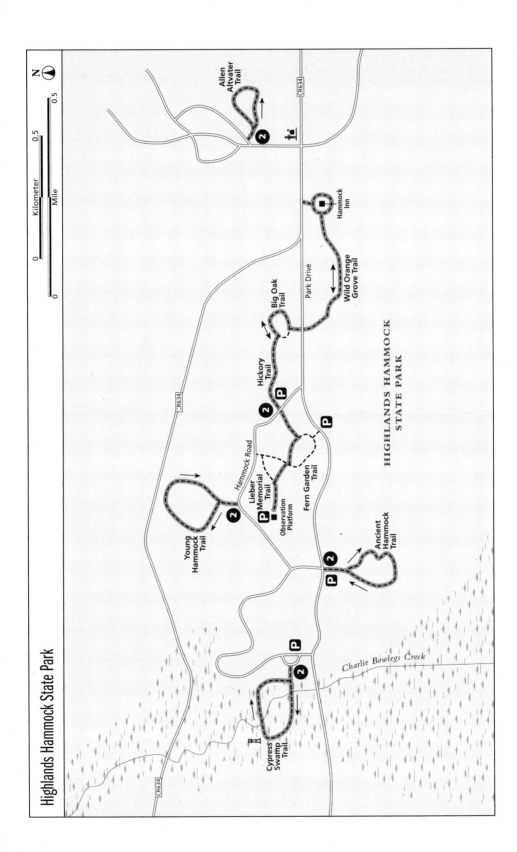

N

0   0.5
Kilometer

0   0.5
Mile

Allen Altvater Trail

CR634

Hammock Inn

Park Drive

Wild Orange Grove Trail

Big Oak Trail

Hickory Trail

CR634

Hammock Road

Young Hammock Trail

Lieber Memorial Trail

Observation Platform

Fern Garden Trail

HIGHLANDS HAMMOCK STATE PARK

Ancient Hammock Trail

Charlie Bowlegs Creek

Cypress Swamp Trail

Fern Garden and Lieber Memorial Trails
GPS: N27 28.352' W081 32.565'

The Hike

The Fern Garden trailhead is located across from the Hickory Trail parking lot. This path enters a thick hammock littered with ferns, including sword ferns. Watch skyward, too, to see birds and to observe air plants growing in the trees. After crossing a bridge, join the Lieber Memorial Trail and a boardwalk into an eerie primal swamp where the dense tree growth blocks most modern sounds. Walk quietly and slowly, and watch. The stillness can be amazing, and unsettling. The trail ends at an observation platform. Depending on sunlight conditions, even digital cameras may need flash for close-up photos. Walking back across the bridge to where the trail forks, go straight for a high and dry return to the trailhead. If you go right, you'll have a more adventurous return across stepping stones but end up back at the same place.

Miles and Directions

0.0 From the Hickory Trail parking lot, cross the road to start the Fern Garden Trail.

0.1 When the trail Ts, go right to begin a short segment of the Fern Garden Trail loop.

0.2 Cross bridge. Take a right then a quick left to join the Lieber Memorial Trail.

0.25 Go left to take the side trail to the observation platform.

0.4 Arrive at observation platform; turn around to retrace steps.

0.8 Arrive back at trailhead.

Young Hammock Trail
GPS: N27 28.398' W081 32.773'

The Hike

The parking area for this hike is 1 mile into the park on Hammock Road. Take an interpretive brochure from the trailhead kiosk. This short walk goes through what is considered a "young" hammock in Highlands Hammock terms, though it may appear older than most you'll see in Florida. The tall slash pines show scars from the days they were used to produce turpentine. You'll also see more wild oranges, which are far more sour than sweet oranges. A lumpy skin (think of welts from bad bee stings) are a trademark of the sour variety, where sweet oranges are smoother.

Miles and Directions

0.0 Start from parking lot.

0.3 Trail passes bench as it curves right.

0.6 Return to trailhead.

Getting wet feet is a normal part of hiking low-lying areas during the summertime rainy season.

Cypress Swamp Trail
GPS: N27 28.301' W081 33.143'

The Hike

The parking area for the Cypress Swamp Trail, probably the park's most popular, is 0.8 mile beyond the Young Hammock Trail. The pathway is a boardwalk that winds among the moss-draped trees spanning both sides of Charlie Bowlegs Creek. You may not think a swamp could possibly be beautiful, but this one certainly is. If possible, make your walk here in late afternoon as the sunlight slants through the trees, casting spooky reflections in the black water covering the swampland. This can be an excellent place for spotting alligators.

Miles and Directions

0.0   Start from parking lot.

0.2   Reach observation platform.

0.4   Return to trailhead.

Ancient Hammock Trail

GPS: N27 28.211' W081 32.916'

The Hike

The trailhead parking lot is located 2.2 miles along Hammock Road, on the right after it loops. Take a footpath leading into a glimpse of the original Florida as you walk beneath a thick canopy of aged live and laurel oaks. The canopy is dense, like that of a rain forest, so that everything turns into a ghostly shadow world. The mature age of these trees is evident as you pass the fallen trunks of giant oaks in several places. The rotting trees, which once supported myriad life forms, now nourish a variety of ferns. Like many of the other short walks here, this is not a path to barge through but to savor and take time to enjoy the sense of wonder.

Miles and Directions

0.0   Start from the Ancient Hammock parking area.

0.2   Pass bench. Go straight.

0.6   Return to parking lot.

Allen Altvater Trail

GPS: N27 28.395' W081 31.823'

The Hike

This is the one walk that doesn't start from Hammock Road. The trailhead is in the main campground, starting across from campsite 115. Park in the space near 114, but do not block any campsite if you'd like to see your vehicle when you return.

This is one of the park's newer trails, created mostly as an activity for campers. Compared to the park's other trails with their concentration of ancient trees, this could be a disappointing walk, yet it does have its own strengths. At the start, older pines have been victim to a pine bark beetle infestation, with the next generation slowly replacing them. Farther along, the sand path penetrates a nice corridor created by gallberry and saw palmetto as the trail loops back toward the campground.

Miles and Directions

0.0   Start from campsite 115.

0.3   Pass benches in clearing.

0.6   Return to parking area.

More Information

Local Information

Sebring Chamber of Commerce: www.sebringflchamber.com.

Highlands County Convention and Visitors Bureau: www.highlandscvb.com.

Local Events/Attractions

The 3-mile road spanning Highlands Hammock is a level loop trail ideal for **bicycling.** Park authorities recognize this and have bikes for rent at the ranger station. Bikes are not allowed on the nature trails; they need to be parked at the respective trailhead. Also available is a 6-mile off-road bike trail.

One-hour **tram tours** (under $5 for adults) venture into remote park areas where you may see alligators, turtles, wading birds, and more. Tours are offered Tuesday through Friday at 1:00 p.m., and Saturday and Sunday at 1:00 p.m. and 2:30 p.m.

The park's renovated **CCC Museum** tells the story of the Civilian Conservation Corps (CCC), which built this and seven other state parks in the 1930s. They did good work because most of their buildings are still in use. They're most remembered here for the 1,450-acre botanical garden they built over six years. It became part of Highlands Hammock in 1941.

Located twenty minutes from Sebring is the 845-acre Lake June in Winter Scrub State Park, also fifteen minutes from historic Lake Placid. Lake June offers **hiking** through rare scrub habitat, including a 0.25-mile nature walk along a spring-fed creek. Several miles of fire lanes also transverse the area. Take US 27 to the town of Lake Placid, turn west on County Road 621, travel approximately 5 miles on CR 621 (Lake June Road) to Daffodil Road (CR 621 merges into Poplar, then into Miller as you travel toward Daffodil). Turn south onto Daffodil Road (Spur Mini Mart is at this intersection). Travel 2 miles to the end of Daffodil Road; the park entrance is on your left. Information is also available at Highlands Hammock State Park and www.floridastateparks.org/lakejuneinwinter, or call (863) 386-6099.

Archbold Biological Station, located south of Lake Placid, is a private **research** facility that studies the rare ecosystem in South Florida; www.archbold-station.org/abs/visitorinfo/visitor.htm.

Both Highlands Hammock and the local community sponsor many different events throughout the area, the majority during the cooler winter and spring months. Check the various Web sites for details. The most famous annual event is the twelve hours of endurance **racing** every March at the Sebring International Raceway, also home of the American Le Mans Series; www.sebringraceway.com.

Lodging

In Sebring: www.highlandscvb.com.

Camping

Highlands Hammock has primitive camping plus 159 developed sites for tents and RVs, most with water and electricity. Advance camping reservations are recommended in winter. Reservations: (800) 326-3521; www.reserveamerica.com/index.jsp.

Organizations

Florida Department of Environmental Protection/Division of Recreation and Parks: www.dep .state.fl.us/parks.

Friends of Highlands Hammock State Park (citizen support organization): 5931 Hammock Road, Sebring, FL 33872.

Hammock Inn (visitor service provider): 5931 Hammock Road, Sebring, FL 33872 (863) 385-4136.

3 Six Mile Cypress Slough Preserve: Boardwalk Trail

From the Six Mile Cypress Slough Preserve boardwalk you'll have a good view of man-made Gator Lake, seasonally popular with wading birds.

Located just south of Fort Myers, this 1.2-mile boardwalk penetrates an otherwise inaccessible 2,200-acre wetland. The slough, measuring 9 miles long and about 0.3 mile wide, is a natural wildlife corridor for white-tailed deer, bobcat, and turkey. Birds often present include ibis, bald eagles, snowy egrets, and warblers. Also look for raccoons and alligators.

Six Mile Cypress Slough (pronounced "slew") and the boardwalk at nearby Corkscrew Swamp (see the next hike in this book) are two of the longest elevated nature trails in the state. In addition to its considerable length, the Cypress Slough boardwalk has two observation platforms and a blind for early morning photography. It passes through a wide variety of natural communities including pine flatwoods, hardwoods, a cypress slough, flag pond, and island hammocks. During summer rains, water depth in the slough averages 2 to 3 feet, making it a wide, shallow stream that eventually flows into the Estero Bay Aquatic Preserve.

The boardwalk is part of a county park also containing picnic and shelter areas, restrooms, and an amphitheater. Free guided walks are offered seasonally.

Nearest town: Fort Myers
Start: 7751 Penzance Boulevard, Fort Myers
Distance: 1.2-mile lollipop loop
Approximate hiking time: 45 to 60 minutes
Difficulty: Easy
Trail surface: Boardwalk
Seasons: Anytime; best wildlife viewing November to March
Other trail users: Hikers only
Canine compatibility: No pets
Land status: County park

Fees and permits: No entrance fee. Hourly parking fee, $5 maximum
Schedule: Open 8:00 a.m. until sunset daily. Guided walks offered daily at 9:30 a.m. and 1:30 p.m. January through March; on Wednesday only at 9:30 a.m. May through October; and daily at 9:30 a.m. in April, November, and December. For reservations, call (239) 432-2040.
Maps: At the trailhead; none needed
Trail contact: Lee County Parks and Recreation at (239) 432-2004; www.leeparks.org/sixmile

Finding the trailhead: From Interstate 75, take exit 136 and go west on Colonial Boulevard. Turn left onto Six Mile Cypress Parkway and go south 3.2 miles to Penzance Boulevard. Turn left onto Penzance Boulevard. The parking area for Six Mile Cypress Slough is almost immediately on the left. **GPS:** N26 34.270' W081 49.567'

The Hike

Covering only 80 acres out of 2,200, the boardwalk still manages to show off an amazing variety of terrain, trees, and plants. At the fringe, it starts in a higher and drier pine flatwoods with sandy soil. This type of terrain is the favorite traveling route for wildlife. The boardwalk soon arrives at a lake and three ponds. The largest body of water is man-made Gator Lake, which was excavated to create the base for a nearby road. It's become a popular feeding area for wading birds. The three ponds— Otter, Wood Duck, and Pop Ash Ponds—are excellent descriptions of what you can hope to find in them, though you'll be fortunate to spot an otter or wood ducks. More likely it will be great and snowy egrets, herons, and white ibis.

▶ **You'll find five observation decks for wildlife viewing along the boardwalk.**

As the elevation drops slightly, you move into a hardwood transition zone where the air may feel slightly different: more humid but also cooler. With the soggier soil unsuited to some types of plant life, the trees here act as the anchors for large numbers of air plants, or epiphytes. The higher up the plants, the easier it is for them to receive sunlight and to disperse their seeds. The most abundant ground plant is the swamp fern.

In the central part of the slough is the open flag pond community where broad leaf fire flags and alligator flags offer hiding places for freshwater fish like bluegill, largemouth bass, catfish, and the oscar, an exotic tropical fish now established in South Florida. Wading birds and osprey frequent this zone as do raccoons and armadillos. The cypress here are not bald but pond cypress, the type that generally forms the characteristic cypress domes.

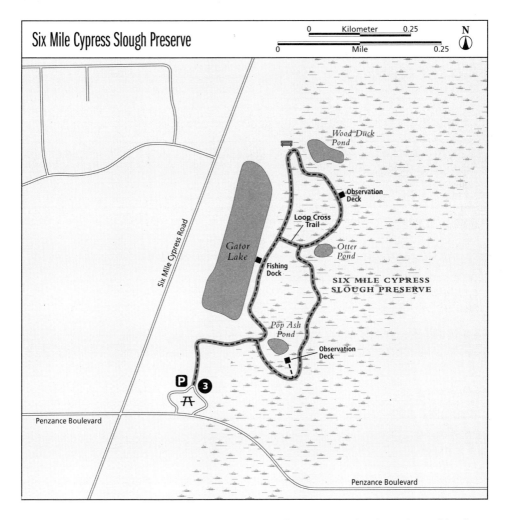

Hammocks, really elevated land patches or islands, permit hardwood trees like the American elm as well as saw palmetto and cabbage palm to grow. These hammocks are especially attractive to snakes; there are fifteen types in the slough, most of which are harmless except for the Florida cottonmouth, sometimes simply called the water moccasin. The brown-colored snakes are heavy bodied and generally grow to around 3 feet, though the record goes to 6. They do not lay eggs but grow the young inside the female in a so-called shell-less egg. Frogs and fish are their main diet.

Overall, mosquitoes aren't much of a problem along the walk thanks to the mosquito fish (gambusia) that tend to keep the population in check. Another fish of note is the sailfin molly with its large dorsal; on the male, the dorsal is orange and blue. These popular aquarium fish are native to Florida but have proven a real pest when released elsewhere, particularly Australia, where a fine up to $150,000 may be levied against someone found with the fish. That's an amazing amount of money, but it shows just how serious the Aussies are about stopping the spread of our sailfin mollies.

Miles and Directions

0.0 Join the boardwalk path at the parking lot.

0.2 Beginning of loop trail. Bear to the left. Return loop comes in from right.

0.3 Loop cross trail comes in from the right. Go straight.

0.8 On the return loop walk, reach junction with opposite end of loop cross trail. Go straight.

1.0 Pass observation deck at Pop Ash Pond.

1.2 Trail ends at parking lot.

More Information

Local Information

Lee County Visitor & Convention Bureau: www.leevcb.com.
Greater Fort Myers Chamber of Commerce: www.fortmyers.org.
Town of Fort Myers: www.fortmyersbeachfl.gov.

Local Events/Attractions

Moonlight walks, bird watching, and summer naturalist camps are just a few of the ongoing **activities** at Six Mile Cypress Slough. For what's happening now: www.leeparks.org/sixmile.

The 105-acre **Calusa Nature Center and Planetarium** in Fort Myers has three nature trails, a museum, planetarium, and butterfly and bird aviaries: (239) 275-3435 or www.calusanature.com.

Four Mile Cove Ecological Preserve in Cape Coral has good **canoe and kayak** waterways: (239) 574-7395.

Babcock Wilderness Adventures in nearby Punta Gorda offers **eco-tours** on its 90,000-acre working ranch and wilderness area. Swamp buggies are the only vehicles that can pass through this section of highlands, marsh, and swamp: (941) 637-0551, (800) 500-5583, or www.babcock wilderness.com.

Lodging

Fort Myers: www.fortmyers-sanibel.com.

Organizations

Lee County Parks & Recreation: www.leeparks.org.
Friends of Six Mile Cypress Slough Preserve: www.sloughpreserve.org.

4 Corkscrew Swamp Sanctuary: Boardwalk Trail

The 2.25-mile boardwalk at Corkscrew Swamp takes you through the world's largest remaining subtropical old-growth bald cypress forest.

The 11,000-acre Corkscrew Swamp, owned and operated by the National Audubon Society, protects the world's largest remaining subtropical old-growth bald cypress forest. This northern tip of the Big Cypress Swamp contains towering bald cypress more than 130 feet high and as much as 700 years old; these are some of the oldest trees in eastern North America.

The Audubon Society began protecting the swamp's great egrets and wood storks from plumage hunters back in 1912. But it wasn't until 1954 that society members began purchasing land to create the preserve. Their actions were timely. Although this was an isolated region back then, development encircles Corkscrew Swamp today.

Yet it is still, as someone once said, "a million years from Miami." Or Orlando, or any other urban area. This is the genuine Florida that existed for thousands of years before man invented plastic pink flamingoes and plaster brown pelicans.

A 2.25-mile boardwalk winds through a world-renowned old-growth forest. The dry winter period is best for wildlife viewing, when wading birds and other animals are forced to concentrate at the feeding pools near the boardwalk, a perfect situation for close-up viewing of birds, alligators, deer, bobcats, and wood storks.

Nearest town: Immokalee
Start: Blair Audubon Center
Distance: 2.25-mile lollipop loop
Approximate hiking time: 2 hours
Difficulty: Easy
Trail surface: Boardwalk
Seasons: January to May, the normal dry season
Other trail users: Nature lovers, photographers
Canine compatibility: No pets

Land status: Private
Fees and permits: Entrance fee of $10
Schedule: For the best birding, be there when the boardwalk opens at 7:00 a.m. It closes at 5:30 p.m. in winter, 7:30 p.m. in summer.
Maps: None needed
Trail contacts: Corkscrew Swamp Sanctuary, 375 Sanctuary Road West, Naples, FL 34120; (239) 348-9151; www.audubon.org/local/ sanctuary/corkscrew

Finding the trailhead: Located off Interstate 75 between Fort Myers and Naples. Take I-75 to exit 111 (Naples Park, County Road 846—formerly exit 17) and go east onto Immokalee Road. (Do NOT take exit 123, Corkscrew Road.) Go about 15 miles and turn left onto Sanctuary Road at the large brown sign. **GPS:** N26 22.456' W081 36.262'

The Hike

The entire 2.25-mile Corkscrew Swamp boardwalk is barrier free and wheelchair accessible. The elevated walkway leads through a wide variety of landscapes, and you're welcome at any time to stop for extended periods to photograph, relax, or just sit and contemplate. Take water; it's the only sustenance you're allowed to take on the boardwalk. Sandwiches and snacks are sold here but must be consumed before setting out (or on the return).

This area was roadless until the 1950s, and Indians, cattlemen, and hunters all had to use canoes, horses, or swamp buggies to travel this extremely wet area. Any high elevation of pines and cabbage palms was usually turned into a camp. The trail passes close to the "Bird Rookery Camp," first used by plumage hunters, then by Audubon wardens beginning in 1912. (The plume camp is just beyond a shortcut trail coming in from the left that allows you to make a shorter loop walk of only a mile. When nesting wood storks are present, everyone must shorten their stroll and take this shortcut in order not to disturb the birds.)

▶ **The nature store has an excellent selection of bird books and field guides.**

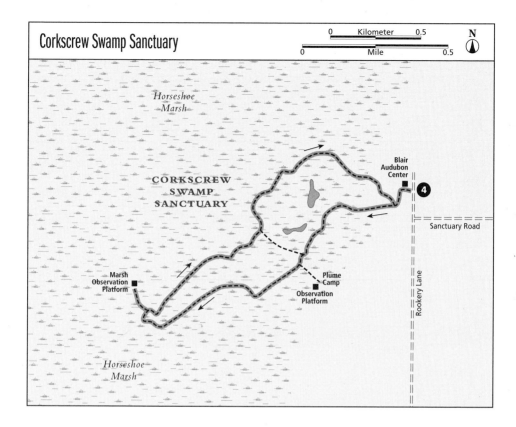

Making the boardwalk circuit, you'll pass through wet prairie that is not wet enough for cypress or dry enough for pines to grow. Instead, grasses and sedges are the dominant vegetation. In spring and summer, the wet prairie is a showcase of wildflowers.

Despite its calm appearance, the swamp water is not stagnant but constantly flowing slowly toward the Gulf of Mexico. During dry periods you may see pools that are scummy due to drought, but they will be flushed and refilled with clean water once the rainy season begins. Ferns are a common and colorful sight throughout the swamp. The swamp fern, which grows to considerable size in the shade, is the most abundant.

Look for the mosquito fish that are so numerous in the swamp water—and thank heaven for them! Mosquito fish feed primarily on mosquito larvae, and that helps keep the mosquito population bearable along the trail.

During winter it's obvious why bald cypress received their name. In the fall, they shed all their leaves and often look lifeless. Although the bald cypress may appear a dingy gray in the bright sunlight, its dark wood is highly valued, which accounts for why virtually all the large cypress stands throughout the country have been cut. The first sections of this boardwalk were made of cypress until it became too scarce. "Lighterwood" pine—highly impregnated with resin and very rot-proof—was used thereafter. The pine is now being replaced by a harder wood expected to last as long as sixty-five to eighty years.

Almost 200 bird species have been recorded in Corkscrew Swamp. You'll probably encounter the largest of Florida's common woodpeckers—the pileated, recognizable by its red crest and black and white pattern. The size of a crow, the pileated woodpecker feeds on beetles and carpenter ants that live inside dead cypress. The bird's loud calls and drumming noises are heard frequently on walks here even though you may never see one.

Miles and Directions

0.0 From the Blair Audubon Center, the boardwalk begins at the back door. Bear left.

0.3 Pass shortcut trail on right. Go left.

0.5 Side trail on left to observation platform at plume camp.

0.7 Pass rain shelter with benches.

1.1 Take side trail on left to marsh observation platform. Retrace steps to main trail. Go left at main trail junction.

1.2 Pass another rain shelter.

1.5 Boardwalk crosses Lettuce Lake, usually a prime alligator viewing spot.

1.6 Shortcut trail comes in from right. Go straight.

1.8 Reach Bypass Trail. Main trail is closed beyond this point during wood stork nesting season.

2.25 Return to Blair Audubon Center.

More Information

Local Information
Greater Naples Marco Island Everglades Convention and Visitors Bureau: www.paradisecoast .com.
Collier County government: www.colliergov.net.

Local Events/Attractions
An extensive calendar of **events** is held every month. Check the Web site for the time you visit: www .audubon.org/local/sanctuary/corkscrew.

A Seminole **reservation and casino** are located in Immokalee.

Lodging
In Naples: www.paradisecoast.com.

Organizations
Audubon of Florida: www.audubonofflorida.org.
National Audubon Society: www.audubon.org.
Collier County Audubon Society: www.collieraudubon.org.

5 Florida Panther National Wildlife Refuge: Duncan Memorial Trail

The yellow warning signs on Everglades-area roads alert drivers that the endangered Florida panther may be present.

Until recently, the 26,400-acre Florida Panther National Wildlife Refuge had been as hard to enter as Fort Knox. Established in 1989 and located 20 miles east of Naples, the refuge has understandably guarded its property closely. So few of Florida's large cats remain in the wild—estimated between sixty to one hundred adults statewide—the refuge was crucial for them to continue to follow their secretive ways.

Comprising 5,000 acres of woodland and 11,400 acres of mixed swamp and prairie, borders of the refuge near highway traffic have high wire fences that rival those of some state prisons. But the fence is not to keep out the public; it's to prevent the great cats from crossing a busy highway and becoming another accident statistic, a too frequent occurrence in the past.

The short Leslie M. Duncan Memorial Trail skirts a hardwood hammock and goes through a pine forest so you have a good chance to keep your feet dry, unless you make the mistake of coming in summer. Remember, this is the Everglades. It's low and supposed to be wet. However, part of the trail at the beginning is elevated and should be wheelchair accessible most of the year.

Nearest town: Immokalee
Start: From the parking lot
Distance: 1.0-mile loop, including 0.3-mile wheelchair-accessible trail
Approximate hiking time: 30 to 45 minutes
Difficulty: Easy unless wet
Trail surface: Natural path
Seasons: Definitely winter, when it's cooler and dryer
Other trail users: Hikers only
Canine compatibility: No pets

Land status: National wildlife refuge
Fees and permits: No fee
Schedule: Open 8:00 a.m. until sunset daily
Maps: Posted at the kiosk; not needed
Trail contacts: Florida Panther National Wildlife Refuge, 3860 Tollgate Boulevard, Suite 300, Naples, FL 34114; (239) 353-8442 or www .fws.gov/floridapanther. The refuge headquarters is not located on site but in East Naples at exit 15 off Interstate 75.

Finding the trailhead: Take I-75 for 20 miles east of Naples. At exit 80, turn left to go north on State Road 29. The hiking trail is on the left about a half mile from I-75. Road signage may be poor, but the signs at the access gate are easily visible. **GPS:** N26 9.89' W081 20.766'

The Hike

Surprisingly, the parking lot here is huge, easily capable of holding tour buses. Everyone wants to see a panther in the wild, but the chances really are slim to none. Not only are there so few of them, but the cats are most active at night. During the day, they rest. On the other hand, you never know, one could appear. And black bear were seen in this region while the trail was being built. Hope springs eternal. If nothing else, this is a nice scenic walk through hardwood hammock and pine flatwoods with good concentrations of wildflowers adjacent to the path.

▶ **To find acceptable prey, a Florida panther may have to walk between 15 and 20 miles a day.**

An estimated five to eleven panthers do use the refuge in a given month, some of them just passing through. Florida panthers need wide ranging areas, and this is one of the largest with some of their preferred habitat. Florida Panther National Wildlife Refuge is in the heart of the Big Cypress Basin, west of the Big Cypress National Preserve and north of the Fakahatchee Strand Preserve State Park and Picayune Strand State Forest. Together, they provide some of Florida's richest panther habitats.

To study home-range size, habitat use, and reproductive success, the Florida Fish and Wildlife Conservation Commission captures and radio-collars panthers. In addition, tracks and scrapes are recorded, and infrared cameras photograph panthers and other wildlife utilizing the refuge, such as black bear, bobcat, and white-tailed deer.

Both the hike and refuge are open during daylight hours only. To keep the cats from

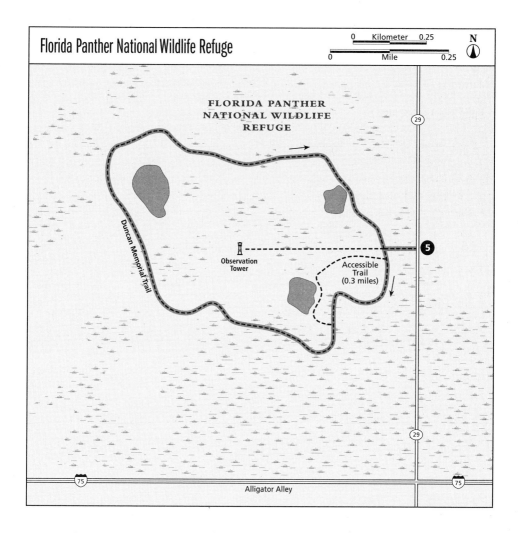

Florida Panther National Wildlife Refuge

FLORIDA PANTHER
NATIONAL WILDLIFE
REFUGE

Duncan Memorial Trail

Observation
Tower

Accessible
Trail
(0.3 miles)

29

5

29

75

Alligator Alley

75

0   Kilometer   0.25

0   Mile   0.25

N

wandering into high-speed traffic, most of the refuge is fenced off. Even the hiking trail itself is fenced off by a high, formidable green fence with two gates. To start the hike, push against the large gate on the left side of the parking lot. This entrance also serves as trailhead for the short nature trail. The gate will automatically spring shut.

The first part, known as the blue trail, is well packed and high and dry. Once you go left onto the red trail, you're joining an old jeep road that's likely to be muddy and, depending on rain, overgrown because the refuge is unable to mow it in wet, soggy conditions. You'll soon come to a clear area where you'll spot a cell phone tower on the right. Bear left to follow the path away from the tower, passing into a burned area and approaching a man-made pond on the right. The pond was made to attract wading and water birds that feed and roost on the refuge. Beyond here the path has a limestone rock base as it enters the pinelands, an excellent area for wildflowers, especially American beauty berries in fall.

Next, you'll walk through a relatively open area of pine flatwood with saw palmettos and return to a more dense hardwood hammock with ferns lining the pathway. This is the most scenic part of the walk. All too soon you're back at another automatic gate at the parking lot, opposite from where you entered.

Miles and Directions

0.0 Leave parking lot; push open large green gate.
0.1 Go left to join red trail.
0.2 Pass cell phone tower. Bear left.
0.5 Enter burn area, pass ponds on right.
0.6 Veer right at red marker.
0.7 Enter hardwood hammock.
0.9 Pass through swinging gate.
1.0 Return to parking lot.

More Information

Local Information
Everglades Area Chamber of Commerce: www.evergladeschamber.com.
Collier County Government: www.colliergov.net.

Local Events/Attractions
The refuge holds several **events** open to the public, usually in winter months: www.fws.gov/floridapanther.

Lodging
Lodging is available in Immokalee or Naples: www.evergladeschamber.com.

Camping
A commercial campground is located in Immokalee.

Organizations
Friends of the Florida Panther Refuge: www.floridapanther.org/index.html.

THE FLORIDA PANTHER

The Florida panther is one of the earth's most endangered animals. Only an estimated eighty to one hundred remain in the wild. This is up from earlier estimates of thirty to fifty animals, but an accurate census is impossible.

A subspecies of what is called a mountain lion, cougar, or puma in other parts of the country, the Florida cat is misnamed because it is not black but tan-colored like other cougars. Early settlers who sighted it at night may have thought it was black. Or the name could be derived from the Greek name for leopard since the cat's young are spotted and the adults lack a mane. Correct or not, panther is the accepted name for Florida's feline. Today, Florida has one of the few cougar populations east of the Mississippi. Most of the rest were hunted to extinction.

The Florida panther's diet includes rabbits, raccoons, wild hogs, birds, armadillos and, when food is scarce, even grasshoppers. Able to sprint up to 35 miles an hour over short distances, a panther usually attacks its prey from ambush. It brings down a deer with a bite that severs the spinal cord at the spot where the neck and head join. A panther may take several days to consume its kill. Between feedings, the cat covers the carcass with leaves and dirt.

Although panthers are quite stealthy when hunting, they are notorious for making a surprising variety of noises. They have been known to chirp, whistle, moan, peep, and growl; kittens, in fact, chirp to communicate with their mother. Some people claim that a panther sometimes makes a cry that will stand a person's hair on end.

The Florida panther is ranked as the world's rarest mammal.

A subspecies of cougar that adapted to local conditions, the Florida panther has several distinctive characteristics: a cowlick in the middle of the back and a crook at the end of the tail. It also is lighter in weight, darker in color, and has smaller feet and longer legs than other cougar subspecies.

Don't look for panthers only in the woods. They are good swimmers and have been sighted swimming rivers as much as a mile wide. There is no recorded case of a panther attack on a person, ever. They shy away from humans. Although panther sightings come in from all over the state, most are discounted. Panthers have definitely been seen in the Eastern Everglades, the Big Cypress Preserve, and the Fakahatchee Strand.

Unfortunately, not even the Everglades is a safe haven for the big cats. A dead panther was found to contain levels of mercury so high they would have been fatal for a human. How mercury is entering the South Florida environment is still not totally understood.

6 Fakahatchee Strand Preserve State Park: Nature Boardwalk

Listen carefully for the sound of the pileated woodpecker on the Fakahatchee Strand Boardwalk. The large birds sometimes are very close to the trail.

The Fakahatchee Strand, about 20 miles long and 3 to 5 miles wide, is the major drainage slough (pronounced "slew") of the southwestern Big Cypress Swamp. It holds the largest stand of native royal palms and the largest concentration and variety of orchids in the United States. Overall, the Fakahatchee Strand is considered to have greater natural significance than anywhere of comparable size in Florida.

The trails once used to cut the virgin cypress here are used for self-guided hikes. Guided swamp walks—where you plunge into the midst of the cypress swamp and expect to get wet—are offered by the park and the Friends of Fakahatchee Strand State Preserve (www.friendsoffakahatchee.org). Hikes on old logging roads that stretch for miles are offered once a week from November through March. Those also can be quite wet. The following description concentrates on the famous 1.2-mile boardwalk located well away from the preserve's main headquarters in Copeland.

Nearest town: Everglades City
Start: Parking area at Big Cypress Bend
Distance: 1.2 miles out and back

Approximate hiking time: 30 to 45 minutes
Difficulty: Easy
Trail surface: Natural path and boardwalk

Seasons: December through March. Mosquitoes are hellish in summer.
Other trail users: Hikers only
Canine compatibility: No pets
Land status: State park
Fees and permits: No fee, no permit needed
Schedule: Boardwalk open sunrise to sunset

Maps: None needed
Trail contacts: Fakahatchee Strand Preserve State Park, P.O. Box 548, Copeland, FL 33926; (239) 695-4593; www.floridastateparks.org/ fakahatcheestrand. The park's headquarters is located on Janes Memorial Scenic Drive, just west of Copeland on State Road 29.

Finding the trailhead: Take U.S. Highway 41 from Miami or Naples. The boardwalk is on the north side of US 41 at Big Cypress Bend, 7 miles west of the junction of US 41 with State Road 29. The location is marked both by a STATE PARK sign and a small Indian village. There is no need to visit the ranger station near Copeland. **GPS:** N25 56.514' W081 28.168'

The Hike

The boardwalk penetrates deep into a virgin cypress swamp with bald cypress, royal palms, and thousands of air plants. Wood stork, otter, black bear, mangrove fox squirrel, and the Everglades mink have all been sighted here, so look sharp.

The walk starts on a dirt access path beside a small Seminole Indian village that is not a tourist park. Keep an eye on the canal to your right where there is a chance of spotting an otter cruising along at its standard 6 mph. A giant pileated woodpecker is also apt to suddenly appear anywhere along this path.

After completing the access path, you'll join a boardwalk into the Big Cypress Swamp, whose topography consists of a smooth, sloping limestone plain. During the rainy season from June through September, water flows over this plain to the mangroves lining the Gulf of Mexico. Channels cut into the limestone by the rainfall are referred to as drainage sloughs. These drainage sloughs are essentially elongated swamp forests that are a marked contrast to the open areas that border them. "Strand" is the local name for such elongated swamps.

▶ Your best chance of ever seeing a ghost orchid in bloom is on a ranger-guided hike at the end of June or July. Call the park's main Copeland office for dates/reservations: (239) 695-4593.

Fakahatchee is home to the fabled ghost orchid, a snow-white orchid found only here and in Cuba. Unless the flower is blooming (usually in July), the flower is nothing but a tangle of roots wrapped around a tree, nothing that looks very special. But orchid collectors highly prize it because so far it has never been successfully raised out of the wild. As a result, orchid poaching has been a real problem here. The book and movie *The Orchid Thief* were based on an actual orchid heist that happened here.

The park does offer trips in summer to see the flowering plants, but a walk to see them is like a descent into all the levels of hell due to the pervasive heat, humidity, and bugs. Those who have seen the orchid in all its glory claim the hardship is worth it.

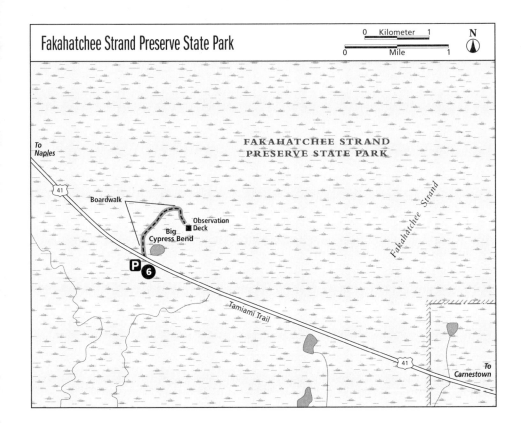

Fakahatchee Strand Preserve State Park

Miles and Directions

0.0 Start from parking lot at Big Cypress Bend.

0.1 Reach boardwalk. Go right.

0.3 Pass cypress trees with large strangler fig attached.

0.4 Pass another large strangler fig.

0.5 Pass over cypress wetlands with pickerel weed and alligator flags.

0.6 Boardwalk ends in an observation deck at the clearwater pond. Sit a spell on the bench before you retrace your steps.

1.1 Boardwalk ends.

1.2 Arrive back at parking lot.

More Information

Local Information

Everglades Area Chamber of Commerce: www.evergladeschamber.com.
Collier County Government: www.colliergov.net.

Local Events/Attractions

Most activities are held in winter months, when mosquitoes and heat are less bothersome.

Swamp walks for a maximum of fifteen are held November through April. With no available paths, you'll wade waist-deep water in the slough and hike for four arduous hours. Long pants and secure footwear are a must. Bring food, water, and insect repellent too.

Three-hour guided **canoe trips** through mangrove tunnels of the East River also are offered November through April. Wading birds, black bears, and even rare crocodiles are all possible sightings. Sun protection, hat, water, and insect repellant are needed.

For dates for either outing, call (239) 695-2440 or visit www.floridastateparks.org/fakahatcheestrand.

For more than three decades, Everglades City has held an annual **seafood festival**, usually in February. Featured foods include gator nuggets, fish chowder, stone crabs, frog legs, catfish fingers, and Indian fry bread: www.evergladesseafoodfestival.com.

Lodging

Everglades City is the closest town. For places to stay, visit www.colliergov.net.

Camping

Collier-Seminole is the closest state park. In Everglades City, Glades Haven RV Park also accepts tenters: (239) 695-2746 or www.gladeshaven.com.

Organizations

Friends of Fakahatchee Strand State Preserve, Inc. (citizen support organization): P.O. Box 35, Everglades City, FL, 34139: www.friendsoffakahatchee.org.

Everglades National Park: Hikes along the Main Road

Everglades National Park is a national treasure as well as Florida's premier wildlife preserve with 2,000 species of plants, 51 types of reptiles, 17 of amphibians, 40 different mammals, and 347 assorted birds. While it is possible to hike the 40-mile road from the visitor center at the main park entrance to Flamingo at the southern tip, few ever do it.

> When the Overseas Railroad was built to Key West in the early 1900s, it entered a part of Florida that had been recently opened for homesteading. Since the railroad work camp at the end of the Florida peninsula didn't have a name, construction materials were sent to the new "Homestead Country," later shortened to "Homestead," the site of today's city.

If making the trek is your goal, do it only in the cooler weather of January and February. To overnight, you must camp along the way. The inn at the end, Flamingo Lodge, is closed as this is written due to storm damage. Hopefully it will reopen in a new, improved incarnation.

Understandably, most people prefer to drive the paved road, stopping periodically at the series of short boardwalks and hiking trails located along the route. Before entering the park, take time to collect all available material at the visitor center and to inspect the selection of books for sale. This is an excellent place to collect a library on the flora and fauna of Florida.

Rangers like to keep the park in its natural state, and that means not changing either the bad or the good. Since mosquitoes are a natural part of the Everglades environment—more so than man—they are allowed to bite whom they want whenever they want; no spraying is conducted. At twilight, be in your tent or in your car unless you want to undergo a profoundly terrible experience. I have never encountered mosquitoes as thick and hungry anywhere else in the world.

Trailheads in Everglades National Park are found in three distinct areas: along the main park road from Homestead to Flamingo; near the Flamingo visitor center and campground; and well away from Homestead in a separate section at Shark Valley off U.S. Highway 41 (Tamiami Trail) 25 miles west of the Florida Turnpike exit for Southwest Eighth Street in Miami.

Nearest town: Florida City
Start: From the main entrance road to Flamingo
Distance: All trails are under a mile
Approximate hiking time: Depends on what you stop to watch and photograph; 30 minutes maximum
Difficulty: Easy
Trail surface: Natural surface and boardwalk
Seasons: December to March is best for weather, mosquitoes, and wildlife viewing—a triple header.
Other trail users: Wildlife photographers, birders
Canine compatibility: No pets
Land status: National park
Fees and permits: Entrance fee $10 per vehicle, good for 7 days at Homestead and Shark Valley entrances
Schedule: Homestead's main park road is

open 24 hours a day (thanks to anglers who launch and return at all hours). Visitor center hours are seasonal. Shark Valley is open 9:15 a.m. to 5:15 p.m.

Maps: Ask at the visitor center or entrance station

Trail contacts: Everglades National Park, 40001 State Road 9336, Homestead, FL 33034; (305) 242-7700; www.nps.gov/ever. Be sure to obtain the latest schedule of ranger-led activities; it is possible to spend an entire day attending one program after another in both the Royal Palm and Flamingo areas. Unfortunately, they are 40 miles apart.

More Information

Local Information
Greater Homestead/Florida City Chamber of Commerce: www.chamberinaction.com.

Lodging
Florida City: Flamingo Lodge is closed.

Camping
Camping is divided into two different categories: frontcountry and backcountry. Frontcountry camping for tents and RVs is available at one of the two developed campgrounds, Long Pine Key and Flamingo. Camping at Long Pine Key is on a first-come basis; reservations for the Flamingo campground can be made at (800) 365-CAMP or www.recreation.gov. Free camping during the wet season—if you can stand not only the damp ground but the hordes of mosquitoes.

Backcountry camping is available on ground and beach sites, though most backcountry sites are on elevated chickees and can be reached only by boat. Contact www.nps.gov/ever/planyourvisit/backcamp.htm.

Organizations
The South Florida National Parks Trust: www.southfloridaparks.org.

The Everglades' shallow sea of grass also contains deep ponds thick with water lilies.

7 Royal Palm Hike: Anhinga Trail

The Anhinga Trail is one of the best places for wildlife viewing in Everglades National Park.

Start: Visitor center
Distance: 0.8-mile loop

Approximate hiking time: 45 minutes

Finding the trailhead: Take State Road 9336 from Homestead to the park entrance. Drive 2 miles and turn left (south) to the Royal Palm Visitor Center. The turnoff is marked, and there are plenty of parking spaces and restrooms open around the clock. The visitor center is open seasonally. The Anhinga Trail starts behind the visitor center. **GPS:** N25 22.951' W080 36.570' (Royal Palm Hammock)

The Hike

Although less than a mile, the Anhinga Trail is probably the park's singular most popular walk. It starts as a paved trail that's actually part of the old highway built in 1916 from Homestead to Flamingo. The narrow ribbon of asphalt leads to a system of boardwalks that loop over a saw grass prairie. They offer superb views of Taylor Slough (pronounced "slew"), one of the best places for wildlife in the park. Polarized sunglasses help in sighting the prehistoric-looking garfish with their narrow streamlined bodies and long snouts. Compared to a garfish, a gator looks positively pleasant. The fish and all the animal life are concentrated in what are actually deep borrow pits created when soil was dug out for road and trail construction. Man's positive influence, for once.

Everglades: Homestead to Flamingo Short Walks

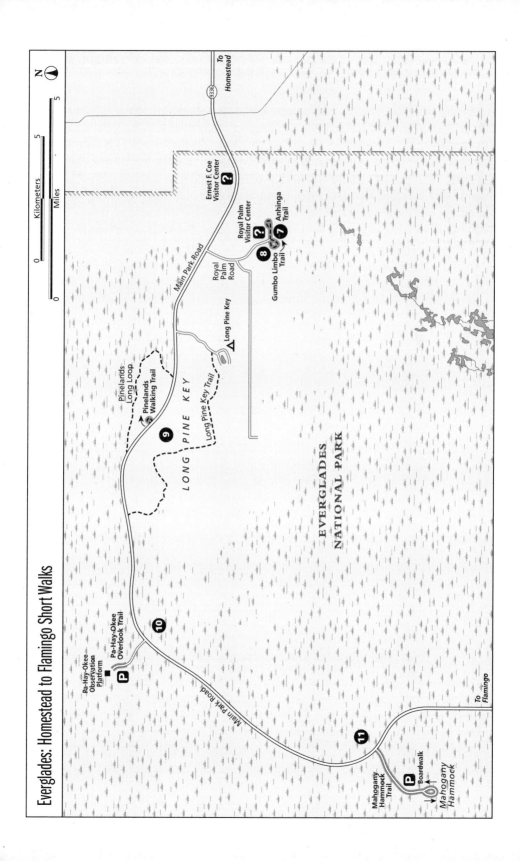

The trail is named for one of the area's most common sights and one of Florida's most distinctive birds. The anhinga, also called water turkey and snake bird, swims almost totally submerged, with only its snaky-looking long neck and head above water. It captures food by diving underwater and spearing fish with its beak, then surfaces and tosses the fish into the air, catches it, and swallows it head first.

Definitely a neat trick, but that's not what makes the anhinga so distinctive. The anhinga is the bird seen sitting on branches with its wings extended like it is in a state of alarm. Actually, the anhinga is drying its feathers because it lacks the oil glands most other water birds have to keep their plumage dry. If the anhinga didn't dry itself regularly, it could get so water-logged it would sink.

Anhingas are alluring, but alligators are arresting. Look for gators in the pond behind the Royal Palm Visitor Center. You may find a big one nearly close enough to touch (but resist the urge if you want to keep your hand!), with just a waist-high stone wall separating you from the reptile. Great pictures! The gators also usually concentrate at the end of the hard pathway where the boardwalk loops into saw grass.

Miles and Directions

0.0 Start from the visitor center. Prepare to turn left to join the paved trail.

0.1 Pass the bench under a tree; beware cormorant fallout. Go straight.

0.2 Pass water gauge and boardwalk coming in from the left; go straight.

0.3 Trail Ys. Boardwalk overlook marks the end of the right path. Go left to take boardwalk into saw grass.

0.4 Spur trail leads to observation overlook. Retrace steps.

0.5 Turn right to rejoin main boardwalk.

0.6 Boardwalk ends at asphalt path. Turn right onto paved path back to visitor center.

0.8 Arrive back at visitor center. Go left to join Gumbo Limbo Trail.

8 Royal Palm Hike: Gumbo Limbo Trail

The red bark of the gumbo limbo tree has earned it the nickname of the "tourist tree," because its peeling layers look like tourists who spend too much time in the sun.

See map on page 51.
Start: Visitor center

Distance: 0.5-mile loop
Approximate hiking time: 30 minutes

Finding the trailhead: Take State Road 9336 from Homestead to the park entrance. Drive 2 miles and turn left to the Royal Palm Visitor Center. The trail starts on the right side of the visitor center. **GPS:** N25 22.951' W080 36.570' (Royal Palm Hammock)

The Hike

A much shorter walk, this totally land-based loop winds through a dense moist forest that is truly jungle-like. The trail is named for the tropical gumbo limbo tree that grows only in South Florida, Cuba, and Hispaniola. The tree has a distinctive red bark that looks like it is constantly peeling; some park rangers call it the "tourist tree" in honor of sunburned visitors.

This trail is one of the most reliable places to look for tree snails. Even a digital camera requires a good flash because of the thick tree cover. The trail wanders among ferns, orchids, air plants, and long trailing woody vines (you can't help but think of Tarzan), all the classic characteristics of a lush Caribbean forest. In places, a thick canopy high overhead dims the sunlight and seems to trap the humidity; bring bug spray.

The effects of past storms on some of the gumbo limbo trees will be demonstrated here for years to come. The winds toppled a number of the trees but did not destroy them. Native to a part of the world where hurricanes frequently occur, gumbo limbo trees survive—even if toppled sideways—by sending out a new root system. The gumbo limbo is a true survivor, and the hurricane's destructive effects graphically demonstrate this.

You'll also find a fascinating geological phenomenon, the solution hole. Erosion caused by wind and rainfall creates a bowl-shaped depression in the limestone bedrock called solution holes, a first step in creating an open collapse sinkhole where water levels are high and the limestone crust thin.

Miles and Directions

0.0 From visitor center, arrive at the Gumbo Limbo trailhead and the start of the loop. Stay right to walk counterclockwise.

0.1 Pass a solution hole on right.

0.2 Pass second solution hole.

0.3 Pass a strangler fig and a bench on the left.

0.4 Boardwalk goes over pond.

0.5 Trail ends, return to visitor center.

9 Pinelands Short Loop

See map on page 51.
Start: Pinelands information kiosk

Distance: 0.4-mile loop
Approximate hiking time: 30 minutes

Finding the trailhead: This trail begins 6 miles from the main visitor center on the main park road to Flamingo. The well-marked turnoff leads to numerous parking spaces, restrooms, and an information kiosk. **GPS:** N25 25.362' W080 40.787'

The Hike

This 0.4-mile trail loops through a forest of slash pines (also called Caribbean or Dade County pine), the only pine species found in the Glades. They grow in a karst landscape known as a rocklands environment. Soft Miami limestone provides the uneven foundation, pocked with numerous solution holes where hard, frequent rains have dissolved the porous rock.

These trees are able to grow here by setting their roots on a key, a Florida term for both hammocks and pinelands where the limestone rock rises above the surrounding wetlands. The pinelands have some of the highest and driest elevation in the park: 3 to 7 feet above sea level.

Slash pines also require very little soil. In many places, the pines are rooted in the potholes that pock the limestone bedrock. Not much space for most trees, but these hollows hold a rich combination of peat and marl.

Pinelands gradually evolve into a hardwood hammock if the area is not periodically burned. Young pine seedlings require plenty of sun to grow, and an unchecked understory of hardwoods will shade them out. Controlled burning, which culls the young hardwoods, leaves the pines sooty but undamaged. The Park Service has used fire since the 1950s to sustain the pinelands.

The Indians practiced the first fire management. They burned the pinelands to ensure that hardwoods did not replace the saw palmetto, which was important in their diet. The palmetto's starchy roots provided the Indians' source of flour.

10 Pa-Hay-Okee Overlook Trail

The Pa-Hay-Okee Boardwalk is one of the best places to appreciate the Everglades' seemingly endless sea of grass.

See map on page 51.
Start: From the parking lot, take the trail on the far right.

Distance: 800 feet out and back
Approximate hiking time: 15 minutes

Finding the trailhead: At 12.1 miles from the park entrance, turn right on the marked turnoff. Proceed 1.3 miles to the parking lot. The trailhead is located just over 12 miles from the visitor center on the road to Flamingo. **GPS:** N25 26.435' W080 47.003'

The Hike

The Pa-Hay-Okee Overlook Trail is a short semicircle that uses an elevated boardwalk leading to a high observation platform with a good view of the immensity of the Glade's saw grass prairie. For as far as you can see, there is nothing but a sea of grass punctuated with scattered, island-like palm hammocks.

Saw grass, one of the oldest plant species in the world, richly deserves its name. But it's better to learn that by sight than from touch. Each grass blade has tiny sharp teeth that discourage animals from grazing on it and help trap water during the dry season. On foggy nights the dew will condense on the plant's teeth and roll down the V-shaped midrib to the roots.

Classified as a sedge *(Caladium jamaicense),* the saw grass extends as a river 100 miles north and south from Lake Okeechobee to the Gulf Mexico, and 50 to 70 miles from east to west. Even during the wettest periods, the average water depth in the Glades is only 6 inches.

You may see an alligator here, but more likely it will be the birdlife that attracts your attention: red-shouldered hawks, red-winged blackbirds, and that most essential scavenger, the vulture. In Florida, vultures are protected by law.

Miles and Directions

0 feet   Depart from parking lot. Take the first trail on the far right at the end of the parking lot.

400 feet   Arrive at the observation platform.

800 feet   Return to parking lot.

11 Mahogany Hammock Trail

The boardwalk through Mahogany Hammock is famous for the strangler figs wrapped so tightly around trees that they have virtually become one.

See map on page 51.
Start: From the parking lot, follow the sign to the boardwalk.

Distance: 0.5-mile lollipop loop
Approximate hiking time: 30 minutes

Finding the trailhead: Drive 19.1 miles from the park entrance; turn right onto the marked road for Mahogany Hammock. **GPS:** N25 19.414' W080 49.925'

The Hike

This boardwalk trail is noted for the nation's largest mahogany tree, with a girth of 12 feet and a height of 90 feet. You start by walking over a wetlands area that forms a Y junction as it enters the hammock. In the cradle of the Y is a short mahogany tree that's become the most recognized symbol of this trail and all the Everglades. The aged tree is notable for the thick network of strangler figs that engulf it.

To see the champion tree, go straight at this junction. The giant mahogany tree is on the left after just a short distance, where the boardwalk suddenly veers left. Mahogany hammocks like this one are rare today in Florida. In the sixteenth and seventeenth centuries, the Spanish cut down most of the mahogany in the nearby Keys. Hard and durable, mahogany has long been highly prized for making furniture and boats.

The hammock can have good bird watching, especially early and late in the day. Woodpeckers are easier to hear than see. Based on the racket they sometimes create in the still quiet, they should all be large, like the pileated woodpecker. Approach them quietly in order not to scare them away or make them move around to the other side of the tree, a favorite trick.

Miles and Directions

0.0 Start from parking lot. Start down the boardwalk almost immediately. The boardwalk soon enters the hammock and comes to the Y junction. Go straight.

0.1 Champion mahogany tree where boardwalk turns left.

0.3 Loop ends. Return to main boardwalk; go right to parking lot.

0.4 Boardwalk ends.

0.5 Arrive back at parking lot.

12 West Lake Mangrove Trail

Start: West Lake turnoff
Distance: 0.4-mile lollipop loop

Approximate hiking time: 30 minutes

Finding the trailhead: Located 30.5 miles into the park on the main park road, 7 miles north of Flamingo. The marked turnoff is on the left. The lake is better known for its canoe trails than its hiking. **GPS:** N25 12.869' W080 51.046'

The Hike

The West Lake Mangrove Trail boardwalk offers a good look at all three types of mangrove forests growing in brackish lakes like this one and on Florida's coasts. The walk here also presents a rare opportunity to see the almost extinct American crocodile.

Mangroves are a vital part of the Everglades ecosystem. They are nurseries for shrimp, crabs, lobsters, and small fish. The tight mangrove roots make wonderful hiding places to protect the tiny marine life from predators. Mosquitoes and mangroves go hand in hand, so take repellent.

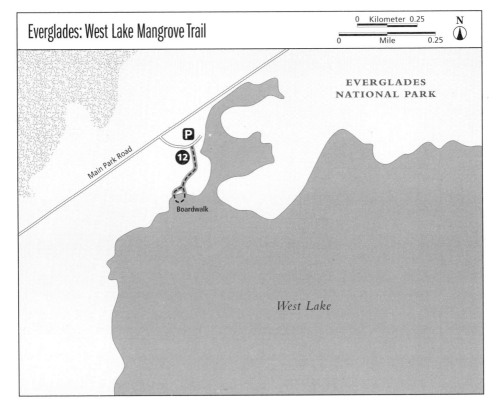

Mangroves also serve as important bird rookeries, secure from most land predators. Raccoons, in search of oysters growing on the mangroves' prop roots, will sometimes dine on birds' eggs instead. Look for bromeliads (air plants) growing in the mangrove branches. Not the normal place for them, but dry habitat is scare here.

In trying to spot a crocodile here, remember that crocs vary in color from greenish to grayish, while alligators are blackish. The most pronounced difference between the two is the head: Crocs have a narrow snout, gators have a broad, blunt one. You'll be fortunate to spot a crocodile, truly a vanishing species: Only a few hundred remain in South Florida, compared to the state's estimated 1.5 million alligators. If you don't spot one here, look for them on the bank behind the marina at Flamingo. In recent years several have shown up each day to sun themselves.

Miles and Directions

0.0 Start from the parking lot.

0.1 Trail forms a T junction. Go left.

0.3 Reach end of loop. Turn left to parking lot.

0.4 Return to parking lot.

Flamingo Area Short Hikes, Hikes 13-14

Trail contacts: Flamingo Visitor Center, (239) 695-2945; www.nps.gov/ever/planyour visit/flam directions.htm. This center is staffed full-time only from November to April.

Once upon a time, this formerly quiet fishing village could be reached only by boats coming across Florida Bay and later through the Homestead-Flamingo Canal. Today, you can drive right up to Flamingo's visitor center and marina at the Everglades' southernmost tip.

Will you see flamingoes at Flamingo? Probably not, although they have been occasionally sighted in Everglades backcountry for the first time in years.

However, on the Flamingo trails you may see unusually bold bobcats who, instead of running away, are little bothered by human presence. It's possible to watch a bobcat fairly closely and for a surprising length of time, even in daylight. Everglades bobcats are just as likely to be found in water as on land, as they search for marsh rabbits, rodents, and birds to feed on.

Flamingo is the gateway to Florida Bay and the coastal prairie. Florida Bay, a huge expanse larger than some states, extends from Flamingo to the Keys. It is incredibly shallow: Parts of it are high and dry at low tide. Nine feet is the maximum recorded depth.

This is ideal habitat for the scores of birds that feed on the mudflats and in the shallows. Look for sandpipers, ospreys, egrets, pelicans, and others.

The magnificent snowy egret once thrived here in such large numbers that in the late 1800s Flamingo became an important center for the trade in bird plumage. Thousands of egrets, roseate spoonbills, and others were killed to supply plumage for women's clothing.

The collecting methods were particularly brutal. Plumage hunters normally waited until the birds were nesting, when the plumage was at its finest and the birds easiest to kill. Hunters would kill all the adult birds in a nest and leave the young to die. The National Audubon Society ended this wholesale slaughter by having the sale of plumage outlawed in New York, headquarters of the fashion industry.

Walking the coastal prairie bordering Florida Bay, you'll see such salt-tolerant plants as mangroves and grasses. You'll notice hardwood hammocks, too, which survive here thanks to the Indian shell mounds that keep their root system high and dry. But you'll find these trees stunted because of the salty, harsh environment.

Flamingo offers eight separate hikes, many quite short. The longer walks (Pinelands Long Loop, Snake Bight/Rowdy Bend Trails, and Bear Lake Trail) are described in the Day and Overnight Hikes section.

13 Eco Pond Trail

Start: Flamingo
Distance: 0.5-mile lollipop loop

Approximate hiking time: 30 minutes

Finding the trailhead: The trailhead is located off the main road just past the Flamingo visitor center at the southern end of State Route 9336. **GPS:** N25 08.322' W080 56.242'

The Hike

This is just a 0.5-mile loop, but it can be loaded with birds and animals. As this is a freshwater pond quite close to Florida Bay, you'll normally see wading birds, songbirds, alligators, and other wildlife. The best bird watching is early and late in the day, from the ramped viewing platform. This is also an exceptional spot for bird photography since this is a popular rookery. The facility was badly damaged by recent storms and, as this is written, still closed; which makes it impossible to identify any significant landmarks along the trail.

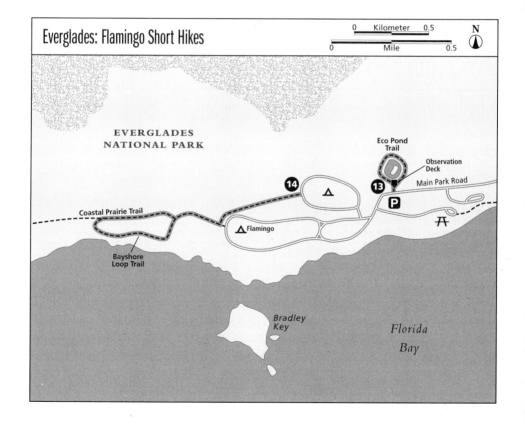

14 Bayshore Loop Trail

The Bayshore Loop Trail starts just beyond the marina at Flamingo. Look behind the marina for the increasing population of saltwater crocodiles.

See map on page 63.
Start: Coastal Prairie Trailhead, Flamingo Campground

Distance: 1.3-mile lollipop loop
Approximate hiking time: 1 hour

Finding the trailhead: The walk begins in the Flamingo Campground south of the visitor center. In the campground, keep bearing right to reach the back of Loop C, and part at the Coastal Prairie trailhead. The Bayshore Loop Trail is a short 1.3-mile segment of the Coastal Prairie Trail, a 7-mile linear trail (14 miles round-trip) that leads to a small primitive campsite. **GPS:** N25 08.213' W080 56.919'

The Hike

The one-hour Bayshore Loop hike leads to the remains of a small fishing village on Florida Bay. You'll start on a leg of the Coastal Prairie Trail, an old cotton picker's path created in the 1930s when the U.S. government decided to eradicate Florida's native wild cotton plants that grow to tree height. The reason: to protect cotton elsewhere in the country because the native Florida cotton contained pink bollworms.

Walking less than a quarter mile, you'll turn left to join the Bayshore Loop, a path of matted vegetation that soon leads to the shores of Florida Bay. Much of your waterside walk will be in the vicinity of mangroves so come prepared, repellant-wise. Look for wading birds up close, hopefully even roseate spoonbills.

Don't expect much in the way of fishing village ruins. The wooden buildings are long gone, though you may be able to find a cistern in the underbrush. Eventually you'll begin to loop back inland and move into an open coastal prairie. When you return to the main Coastal Prairie Trail, go right to return to the parking lot.

If you'd prefer to go left and walk Everglades Park's longest trail, you'll need a backcountry camping permit from the Flamingo visitor center. Or check at the Homestead center when you first enter in case Flamingo's facility is closed.

Miles and Directions

0.0 Start from the Coastal Prairie Trailhead.

0.2 Turn left to join Bayshore Loop Trail.

0.4 Reach Florida Bay; bear right.

0.7 Trail begins to loop away from shoreline.

0.8 Junction with Coastal Prairie Trail; go right.

1.1 Arrive at beginning of Bayshore Loop Trail coming in from right. Go left to return to parking area.

1.3 Arrive back at parking area.

Eco Pond has long been a popular nesting area for white egrets.

15 Shark Valley: Bobcat Boardwalk and Otter Cave Hammock Trail

Shark Valley is in the northernmost sector of Everglades National Park in a location far from both Homestead and Flamingo. Although Shark Valley is not as well known as other regions in the park, its 15-mile long, hard-surfaced tram road loops deep into the wilderness, making it a prime wildlife viewing area. It's possible to hike or cycle the path, but most visitors explore it by motorized tram, which runs from December 1 to April 1.

Beginning on the hour, from 9:00 a.m. almost until closing, the park operates a two-hour tram ride along the road for less mobile visitors to see the birds, gators, deer, turtles, and other animals. At the end of the road is a 50-foot high observation tower with a panoramic view deep into the Glades. Making the return loop, the tram travels another ruler-straight route paralleling the other side, but the scenery is totally different on the trip back. Since bikes are popular rentals here, hikers who decide to walk the entire length are bound to see quite a few other people.

Just a short distance from the Shark Valley Visitor Center are two short walking trails through habitat common to Everglades: bayheads and hardwood hammocks. You'll start out by walking the main tram road before detouring to walk these less traveled paths.

Start: Visitor center
Distance: 1.5-mile double loop
Approximate hiking time: 45–60 minutes

Trail contact: Call the Shark Valley park office at (305) 221-8776 or visit www.nps.gov/ever/planyourvisit/svdirections.htm.

Finding the trailhead: From Homestead take the Florida Turnpike to the U.S. Highway 41 exit, then go west. The entrance to this park section is 30 miles west of Miami, on the left (south) side of US 41, adjacent to the Miccosukee Indian Village. The trailhead is about 100 yards from the visitor center following the paved tram road. **GPS:** N25 45.348' W080 45.984'

The Hike

Leaving the visitor center, take the left section of the tram road toward the Bobcat Boardwalk. Turning right off the tram road, the Bobcat Boardwalk route itself is only about 500 yards long. It starts out going through a saw grass prairie with extensive cattails, then enters a lowland hammock of willows and other tree species that can survive wet conditions. Interpretive signs identify various plants and ecosystems. When you come out on the opposite side and arrive at the tram road, go left.

The Otter Cave Hammock Trail is a rough, limestone trail only about 200 yards long. It penetrates a hardwood hammock of Caribbean- and Bahamian-type trees

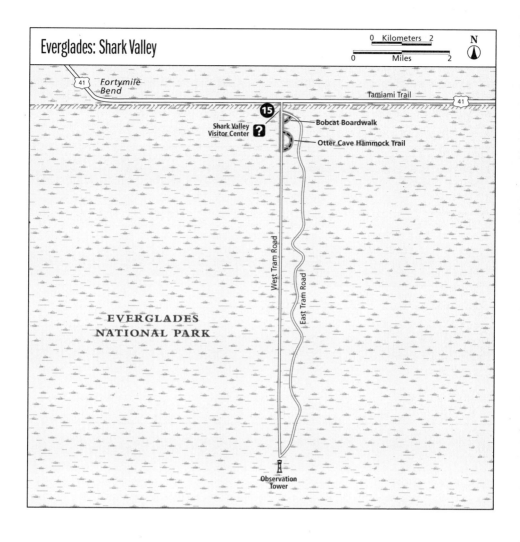

including gumbo limbo and strangler fig (a huge strangler fig is marked by a sign). Following Hurricane Andrew, this area is more open, which is allowing new growth to emerge. As a loop road, this trail returns to the tram road, the side you first walked down to reach the Bobcat Boardwalk. If you don't pay close attention to the signs/markers here, you could become disoriented and mistakenly walk toward the distant observation tower instead of quickly returning to the visitor center.

Miles and Directions

0.0 Depart from visitor center, going left on the paved tram road (East Tram Road).

0.1 Turn right to join Bobcat Boardwalk.

0.4 Arrive at opposite end of boardwalk on West Tram Road. (**Option:** To return to visitor center, go right.) To reach nearby Otter Cave Hammock Trail, turn left (south).

0.5 Arrive at the Otter Cave Hammock Trailhead; go left (east) to walk loop clockwise.

0.75 Complete trail, return to paved West Tram Road. Go right (north) to return to Shark Valley Visitor Center.

1.5 Arrive back at Shark Valley Visitor Center.

Boardwalks are the only feasible way to penetrate the wet, thick grassy areas of the Everglades.

16 Loxahatchee National Wildlife Refuge: Cypress Swamp Boardwalk

The Cypress Swamp Boardwalk at the Loxahatchee NWR is one of South Florida's most scenic boardwalks. The swamp houses numerous giant leather ferns.

South Florida has many nature boardwalks, but to me Cypress Swamp Boardwalk is one of the most scenic as well as one of the best for spotting wildlife. What makes this cypress swamp so special is the heavy concentration of giant leather ferns, the largest fern in North America. Growing up to 14 feet tall, they do deserve their "leather" name. Examine the underside of a fertile frond: The rust-brown spores covering the underside do indeed look like suede leather.

Alligators are often out sunning in the ponds in front of the Cypress Swamp Boardwalk at the visitor center. Wading birds and turtles are also common. And don't overlook the butterfly garden in the parking lot, where black and yellow striped zebra long-winged butterflies constantly feed.

The swamp boardwalk represents only a sliver of the 147,392-acre Arthur R. Marshall Loxahatchee National Wildlife Refuge. The nature walk may whet your appetite for more. Just down the road is a longer day hike around a series of impoundments that attract wintering waterfowl. Ask for a map at the visitor center.

Nearest town: Delray Beach
Start: On the right-hand side of the visitor center
Distance: 0.45-mile loop
Approximate hiking time: 30 minutes
Difficulty: Easy
Trail surface: Wood boardwalk
Seasons: Fall through spring
Other trail users: Hikers only
Canine compatibility: No pets

Land status: National wildlife refuge
Fees and permits: Day use fee under $5
Schedule: Open daily from sunrise to sunset.
Maps: None needed
Trail contacts: Arthur R. Marshall Loxahatchee National Wildlife Refuge, 10216 Lee Road, Boynton Beach, FL 33437; (561) 734-8303; www.fws.gov/loxahatchee. Once in the Palm Beach area, tune your radio to 530 AM for the latest Loxahatchee information.

Finding the trailhead: Many different routes lead here. From the South via Interstate 95: Take I-95 north to Atlantic Avenue/State Road 806 and go left. Travel west on Atlantic Avenue/SR 806 about 7.5 miles to State Road 7/U.S. Highway 441 and turn right. Travel north 3.1 miles to Lee Road and turn left. Travel west 0.3 mile to the Loxahatchee National Wildlife Refuge.

From the South via Florida Turnpike: Take Florida Turnpike north to Atlantic Avenue/SR 806 and go left. Travel west 7.5 miles on Atlantic Avenue/SR 806 to SR 7/US 441 and turn right. Travel north 3.1 miles to Lee Road and turn left. Travel west 0.3 mile to the refuge.

From the North via I-95: Take I-95 south to State Road 804/Boynton Beach Boulevard. Keep right at the fork in the ramp but be prepared for a left turn onto SR 804/Boynton Beach. Travel west 8.5 miles to SR 7/US 441 and turn left. Travel south 2 miles to Lee Road and turn right. Travel west 0.3 mile to the refuge.

From the North via Florida Turnpike: Take Florida Turnpike south to SR 804/Boynton Beach Boulevard. Keep right at the fork in the ramp, then turn left onto SR 804/Boynton Beach Boulevard. Travel west 8.5 miles to SR 7/US 441 and turn left. Travel south 2 miles to Lee Road and turn right. Travel west 0.3 mile to the refuge.

The visitor center and its boardwalk are just inside the park, on the right. **GPS:** N26 29.961' W080 12.721'

The Hike

The boardwalk behind the visitor center penetrates a dense cypress swamp that is truly eerie in its stillness and closeness. One of the more remarkable sights here is the tremendous number of air plants rooted to the trees. They are attached to the skinny cypress trunks and branches one after another, like decorations on a Christmas tree.

▶ **Arthur R. Marshall was a scientist and Everglades conservationist who, along with Marjory Stoneman Douglas, helped stop a jetport in the Everglades and cancel the completion of the Cross-Florida Barge Canal.**

The air plants, or epiphytes, are among the most interesting plants in the Everglades. They are nonparasitic and use their roots only as anchors. Because of the alternating cycle of drought and high humidity, many of them have tough skins to reduce moisture loss while others have thick stems in which to store it. Many are shaped to collect water at their bases. When blooming,

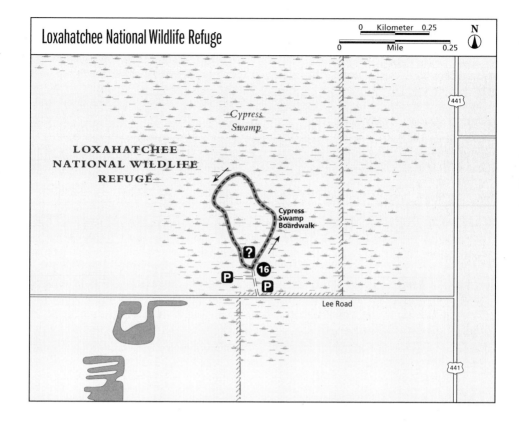

the cardinal air plant displays bright red bracts that almost hide the small purple and yellow flower inside.

Spanish moss, the gray mats of stringy hair that drape from the cypress, is another epiphyte. They obtain their nutrients from decomposing plant and insect matter that falls on them and from moisture in the air, nothing from their host tree.

Leather ferns may be the most obvious ferns here, but others thrive here, too, including sword, shield, strap, royal, and swamp ferns. Plants dominate the landscape, but look for snakes (sometimes sunning on the boardwalk), bobcats, raccoons, and river otters. Common birds are Carolina wrens, common yellowthroats, cardinals, and red-bellied and pileated woodpeckers.

Miles and Directions

0.0 Depart from the visitor center. Turn left to join the boardwalk. Go straight.

0.2 Pass a bench.

0.3 Pass a bench.

0.45 Boardwalk ends and you'll return to the parking lot.

More Information

Local Information

Palm Beach County Convention and Visitors Bureau: www.palmbeachfl.com.
Palm Beach County Government/Board of County Commissioners: www.co.palm-beach.fl.us.

Local Events/Attractions

Loxahatchee National Wildlife Refuge has an extensive series of events every month. Check the Web site under News & Happenings: www.fws.gov/loxahatchee.

Lodging

In Delray Beach; Greater Delray Beach Chamber of Commerce: www.delraybeach.com.

Camping

No camping facilities are on site. Most campgrounds are for RVs but there are two KOAs in Palm Beach County.

Organizations

U.S. Fish and Wildlife Service Southeast Region: www.fws.gov/southeast.
Friends of Loxahatchee: www.loxahatcheefriends.com.
Arthur R. Marshall Foundation: www.artmarshall.org.

17 J.W. Corbett Wildlife Management Area: Hungryland Boardwalk and Trail

Look for swamp lilies in the wet areas bordering the Hungryland Boardwalk.

The 1.2-mile Hungryland Boardwalk and Trail provides a good, capsulated look of the massive 60,228-acre J.W. Corbett Wildlife Management Area. A natural path links to a series of boardwalks to pass through pine flatwoods, saw grass marsh, an oak/cabbage palm hammock, and a cypress swamp. Along the trail you could see white-tailed deer or bobcats, river otters, raccoons, pileated woodpeckers, barred owls, screech owls, herons, egrets, and common yellowthroats. Interpretive signs mark the trail.

The trail goes through an edge of Hungryland Slough (pronounced "slew"), a shallow basin of slow-moving water populated with cypress domes and open grassy meadows. Surface water remains for long periods of time due to heavy summer rains and slow runoff. This creates ideal humid conditions for not only cypress and pond apples but a profusion of bromeliads and ferns.

Nearest town: Indiantown
Start: Everglades Youth Conservation Camp
Distance: 1.2-mile loop

Approximate hiking time: 45 to 90 minutes
Difficulty: Easy
Trail surface: Natural surface, boardwalk

Seasons: Fall through early spring; a public hunting area September to April
Other trail users: Hikers only
Canine compatibility: Leashed pets permitted
Land status: Wildlife management area
Fees and permits: Daily use permit required (under $5); available at sporting goods stores and county tax offices
Schedule: Open daylight hours
Maps: Posted at the trailhead kiosk

Trail contact: The Florida Fish and Wildlife Conservation Commission: (561) 625-5122; www.myfwc.com/recreation/jw_corbett
Special considerations: This is a public hunting area. During hunts, hikers should wear 500 square inches of blaze-orange clothing above the waist, and it must be visible in both front and back. Hunting schedule is available at www.myfwc.com/hunting.

Finding the trailhead: From Interstate 95 in West Palm Beach, take the Northlake Boulevard exit. Drive west approximately 12.3 miles, crossing the Beeline Expressway (State Road 710). Take a right onto Seminole Pratt Whitney Road. The J. W. Corbett Wildlife Management Area entrance is just ahead. Follow the signs to the Hungryland Boardwalk and Trail, 0.7 mile from the check station, in a grassy parking area. **GPS:** N26 51.350' W080 18.167'

The Hike

Start from a grassy parking lot and go right to join this nature trail. If you go to the far left end of this same parking lot, you'll find the trailhead for a section of the Florida Trail that is also part of the still-developing 65-mile-long Ocean to Lake Trail extending from Hobe Sound to Lake Okeechobee. A part of this trail is described in J. W. Corbett WMA Florida Trail Segment under Long Haulers later in this book.

Though there is little to indicate it, this is a surprisingly historic area and several explanations exist about how this became known as the "Hungryland." According to most state sources, what is now the Corbett WMA appealed to Native Americans as long as 2,000 years ago. Indians dug canals through the saw grass to visit their villages and built several large mound areas where they disposed of their debris and buried their dead. One is the 143-acre site called the Great Mound, a complex of twenty-three mounds with radiating causeways leading to man-made lakes.

▶ **Consider spending time at one of several semicircular ponds that offer both bird watching and freshwater fishing (license required).**

The race that built this culture was quickly killed off by diseases introduced by the Europeans and that the Indians had no resistance against. So this was not a very productive area when the newly arrived Seminole Indians chose a slough here as a hiding place from the U.S. Army during the Seminole Indian War of 1835. It was the wrong choice, and hundreds of starving Indians eventually surrendered and were sent to Oklahoma. Local ranchers named this "The Hungryland." Some Palm Beach County authorities espouse a different version, believing settlers called this the "hungry land" due to infertile soil and the lack of game animals.

Whatever the name source, the boardwalk and nature trail reveal a section seemingly as rich as any in Florida. Yet it is not in its original state. Most of the lumber here

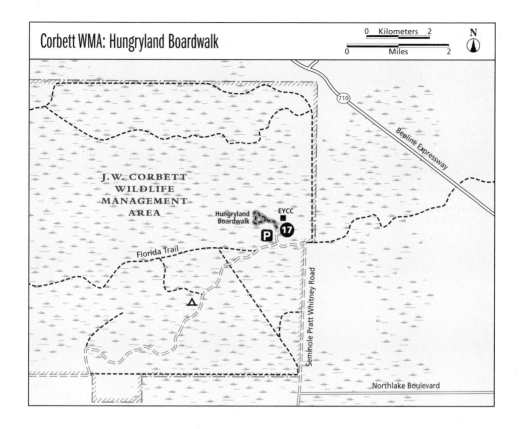

Corbett WMA: Hungryland Boardwalk

0 Kilometers 2

0 Miles 2

N

J. W. CORBETT
WILDLIFE
MANAGEMENT
AREA

Hungryland
Boardwalk

EYCC

P 17

Florida Trail

Seminole Pratt Whitney Road

Northlake Boulevard

Beeline Expressway

710

was timbered in the 1940s, and cattle roamed here before the logging. But this second growth forest is beginning to reach the state where it probably somewhat resembles its previous state, and wildlife is certainly returning.

The boardwalk and natural path are well away from the hunting section, so animals are naturally drawn here. Deer are not obvious, but feral hogs leave their rooting at many points along the natural path. Bobcats appear early and late in the day while river otters and raccoons may appear anytime. In the marshlands near the end of the walk, look for herons, egrets, and common yellowthroats.

Miles and Directions

0.0 From the middle of the grassy parking lot, go right to the Hungryland Trail.

0.1 Natural path ends. Go straight to join boardwalk that crosses an "edge," where two habitats meet and that wildlife uses as a corridor.

0.2 Information kiosk and bench.

0.25 Trail turns right.

0.3 Join second boardwalk that zigzags around trees.

0.6 Boardwalk ends. Natural path leads through palmetto corridor. Go left at bench.

0.7   Boardwalk begins again.

0.8   Boardwalk ends. Take the return path on left.

0.9   Pass information kiosk and bench.

1.0   Cross final boardwalk.

1.2   Arrive back at parking lot.

More Information

Local Information
Palm Beach County Convention and Visitors Bureau: www.palmbeachfl.com.

Lodging
Lodging is available at Indiantown (10 miles north), West Palm Beach (25 miles southeast), and Jupiter (15 miles east).

Camping
Two primitive campsites are located on the Florida Trail, at Miles 5 and 11. A permit is required to stay overnight at the campsites, and fires can be built only in designated areas.

Organizations
Florida Fish and Wildlife Conservation Commission: www.myfwc.com/recreation/jw_corbett.

Day and Overnight Hikes

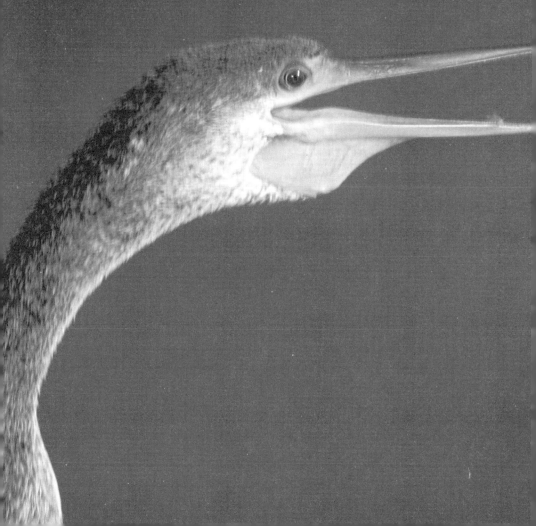

Oscar Scherer State Park: Yellow, Blue, Red, and Green Trails

Heed the warning of this sign at the lake near the nature center at Oscar Scherer State Park.

The 1,384-acre Oscar Scherer Park is restoring a large area of scrubby flatwoods, making this park one of the best places to see the threatened Florida scrub jay. Almost a foot long from beak to tail and with bright blue feathers, the scrub jay is one of the state's most interesting and attractive birds. A member of the crow family, scrub jays are common throughout the southwestern United States; east of the Mississippi they live only in Florida.

As the name implies, scrub jays live around the thickets of short bushy oaks known as scrub. They feed on acorns and, just like squirrels, sometimes bury the acorns for future use. Scrub jays are wary when feeding. Normally one bird will act as a sentinel while the others eat. Yet scrub jays also become quite accustomed to people and often visit the most heavily used parts of the park. Hiking is a specialty here, with four major trails and two short nature trails.

◀ *The long-necked anhinga is a noisy bird that makes a raspy croaking sound.*

Nearest town: Osprey
Start: At the respective trailheads
Distance: Varying hikes up to 5 miles
Approximate hiking time: Longest hike takes 2.5 hours
Difficulty: Easy to moderate
Trail surface: Mostly natural surface
Seasons: December to April
Other trail users: Mountain bikers

Canine compatibility: Pets must be leashed
Land status: State park
Fees and permits: Entrance fee under $5
Schedule: Open 8:00 a.m. until sunset daily
Maps: Available at the trailheads
Trail contact: Oscar Scherer State Park, 1843 South Tamiami Trail, Osprey, FL 34229; (941) 483-5956; www.floridastateparks.org/oscarscherer

Finding the trailhead: The park is located on U.S. Highway 41, 2 miles south of the town of Osprey and 1.7 miles north of State Road 681 between Nokomis and Osprey. Most of the hikes start near the parking lot at Lake Osprey and the adjacent Nature Center, both situated about a mile from the entrance station. A single **GPS** location (N27 10.503' W082 27.718') suffices for referencing the trailheads for all the following hikes.

More Information

Local Information

Sarasota County Chamber of Commerce: www.sarasotachamber.com.
Sarasota County Government: www.co.sarasota.fl.us.

Local Events/Attractions

Canoe or kayak South Creek; rentals available with guided tours Wednesday afternoons.

Extensive **cycling** trails cover 15 miles. A mountain bike is needed to navigate the fine sugar sand. Freshwater **fishing** is available in three-acre Lake Osprey while South Creek holds saltwater species.

The park has two **nature trails** in addition to the main hiking trails. The Lester Finley Trail is a 0.5-mile barrier-free trail that goes through a hardwood hammock along a tidal reach of South Creek. It has a wheelchair-accessible fishing pier, two butterfly gardens, several benches, two picnic tables, and a water fountain along the well-canopied trail. The trail is open to foot traffic only. The 0.5-mile South Creek Nature Trail can be accessed at the picnic area across from the Nature Center or at the South Creek parking lot. It follows South Creek and crosses the road leading into the Campground. It can be combined with the Lester Finley Trail for an easy hike of 1.5 miles and is open to foot traffic only.

Camping

Campsites available for tent or RVs with hook-ups for electric and water. For reservations call (800) 326-3521 or visit www.reserveamerica.com/index.jsp.

Organizations

Friends of Oscar Scherer Park, Inc. (citizen support organization): 1843 South Tamiami Trail, Osprey, FL 34229.

18 Yellow Trail

Start: Marked trailhead across from the parking lot

Distance: 5.0-mile lollipop loop

Approximate hiking time: 2.5 hours

The Hike

The Yellow Trail path passes through mesic pine flatwoods, prairie hammocks, and scrubby flatwoods. It starts in an area that was once prime scrub jay habitat, but the native scrubby flatwoods cleared in the 1940s and replaced with slash pine are being restored. The slash pines are being removed selectively, and prescribed burning is also important in bringing back the scrubby flatwoods, with small oaks, scattered pines, and partial ground cover.

Next, you'll cross a Rails to Trails path and enter the Mary Thaxton Memorial Preserve, another area being returned to scrubby flatwoods. Besides scrub jays, this habitat is a favorite of gopher tortoises and indigo snakes as well as white-tailed deer and turkeys. Bobcats have been sighted along the trail, which also passes through oak hammocks and pine forest. Several bridges are needed to take you past Big Lake, a good spot for wading birds. Returning to the trailhead, you'll pass through a shaded hammock and a recharge area for South Creek, which is fed by draining rain water.

This sandy, level trail can be subdivided into shorter segments of 2.5 and 3.5 miles by taking the indicated shortcuts. Biking is permitted here but often difficult in the soft sand. Stay with the yellow markers. Do not stray onto the Blue Trail, covered below.

Miles and Directions

0.0 Start at trailhead across from parking area.

0.3 Trail turns right at bench 1.

0.5 Turn left at trail junction.

1.0 Pass bench 2.

2.0 Pass bench 4A.

2.5 Pass bench 5; trail turns right.

3.0 Pass bench 6 and shortcut trail coming in from right; go straight.

4.0 Cross bridge.

4.5 Turn left to return to trailhead.

5.0 Trail ends at kiosk.

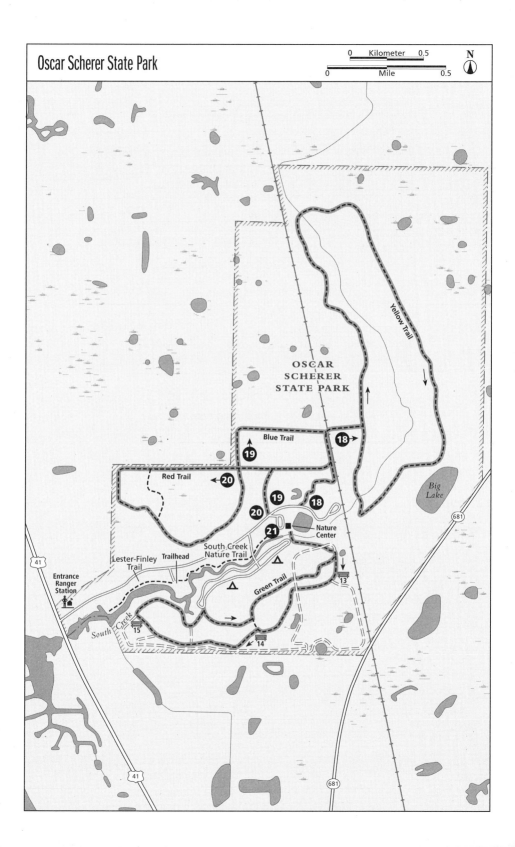

19 Blue Trail

Watch for the purple fruit of the American beautyberry from August to November; it's a favorite of many birds. The plant was used by the Seminole Indians for such medicinal purposes as malarial fevers, rheumatism, dizziness, and stomachaches.

See map on page 81.
Start: Lake Osprey picnic area

Distance: 1.5-mile lollipop loop
Approximate hiking time: 1 hour

The Hike

This hike also passes through scrub jay habitat as it passes through mesic pine flat-woods and scrubby flatwoods. This is a dry open area with lots of sand, which makes biking difficult in spots. The hike begins at the same trailhead as the Red Trail, which it shares for the first 0.5 mile. Then the Blue Trail goes right and after 0.5 mile turns right again to follow a hard-packed road until it meets the Yellow Trail and runs parallel to the Rails to Trails path. After a mile the path turns right, then left at bench 9 before returning to the trailhead.

Miles and Directions

0.0 Start from the Lake Osprey picnic area.

0.2 T junction. Go left.

0.3 Turn right at bench.

0.5 Trail turns right at bench 10.

1.0 Trail turns right.

1.3 Trail turns left to return to parking lot.

1.5 Return to trailhead at Lake Osprey picnic area.

20 Red Trail

The great blue heron is the largest North American heron.

See map on page 81.
Start: Lake Osprey picnic area

Distance: 2.0-mile lollipop loop
Approximate hiking time: 1 hour

The Hike

The best opportunity for wildlife viewing occurs after the trail veers away from the homes and moves toward South Creek. Don't be lured off the main path by any of the service roads you pass; stay on the trail. As in most areas, birds are the predominant wildlife. Great horned owls live in the slash pines near the trail, with their newborn most easily visible in March. In addition to the scrub jays and sand hill cranes that also favor the area are the chuck-will's-widow, a nocturnal bird you may see close to sunset. Once you hear the bird's distinctive call, it's obvious how the bird received its name. It does cry a loud "Chuck-will's-widow," though the first "chuck" being quiet and inaudible at a distance.

The Red Trail shares the trailhead and its path with the Blue Trail at the beginning and then splits off to follow the park boundary beside a housing development. The trail is also open to cycling, though it can be difficult for bikes in spots. A short-cut can reduce the hike to 1.5 miles.

Miles and Directions

0.0 Start from the Lake Osprey picnic area.

0.2 T junction. Go left.

0.3 Blue Trail turns right at bench. Continue straight.

0.5 Shortcut comes in from the left. Continue straight.

1.0 Opposite end of shortcut comes in from the left. Continue straight.

1.7 Trail Ts. Go right to return to trailhead.

1.8 Go right to return to trailhead.

2.0 Arrive back at trailhead at Lake Osprey picnic area.

21 Green Trail

See map on page 81.
Start: Behind the Nature Center

Distance: 3.0-mile lollipop loop
Approximate hiking time: 1.5 hours

The Green Trail will take you through scrubby flatwoods and mesic pine flatwoods. It is considered the best biking trail in the park.

At the start, the path crosses South Creek by bridge and leads to the campground. After passing several campsites, it follows an unpaved road that leads to a gate. Any chain is to block motorized vehicles. Walk around it to enter Florida scrub jay habitat with little tree canopy.

Just beyond the gate at bench 13 you can take an unpaved road of about a mile that rejoins the Green Trail. This side trail goes through pine flatwoods where gopher tortoises are common. The slash pines still show evidence of the turpentine industry of the early 1900s when the bark was exposed so sticky resin could be collected.

▶ **Oscar Scherer (1856–1923) invented a process for dyeing shoe leather in 1872. His daughter left the family's South Creek Ranch to the state, which was the basis for the park.**

The southern segment of the Green Trail parallels a housing development before turning right to border South Creek and returning to the Nature Center. It can be shortened to a 2-mile hike.

Miles and Directions

0.0 Start from behind the Nature Center.

0.3 Walk around gate. Bear to the right. Continue straight as Green Trail comes in from the right.

0.5 Arrive at bench 13. Green Trail bears right. Optional side road goes left.

0.7 Optional side trail rejoins Green Trail from the left.

1.0 Arrive at bench 14. The shortcut trail coming in from the right shortens the hike to 2 miles. Continue straight to complete the Green Trail.

1.5 Trail turns right at bench 15.

2.0 Trail makes a sharp right at gate.

2.5 Trail crosses unpaved road; go straight.

2.8 Return to trail access gate. Go around and turn left to return to Nature Center.

3.0 Arrive back at Nature Center.

Ding Darling National Wildlife Refuge

The 850,000 people who annually tour the 6,354-acre J. N. "Ding" Darling National Wildlife Refuge do so by car, though biking and walking offer a slower pace in which to enjoy this area and to view wildlife. Also, it's quite easy to walk the 5-mile Wildlife Drive atop a mosquito control dike that passes through mangrove forests and tidal pools.

Ding Darling is famous for its large flocks of wintering waterfowl, most plentiful from January through March. The rest of the year, look for herons, egrets, plovers, and ibis stalking the mud flats in search of shrimp, marine worms, aquatic insects, and other tidbits. Alligators, too, of course. With 2,825 acres of the refuge (over a third) designated as a Wilderness Area, it's not surprising this coastal refuge is so wildlife rich: 238 bird species (seasonal) as well as 51 reptile and amphibian types and 32 mammal species. Threatened and endangered species include eastern indigo snakes, American crocodiles, bald eagles, wood storks, peregrine falcons, West Indian manatees, and Atlantic loggerhead turtles.

▶ **Sanibel is world famous for its excellent shelling, which is at its best following fall and winter storms when waves push thousands of shells onto the beach. It's possible to find many varieties of shells, but probably the most sought-after is the Florida horse conch, a huge orange shell large enough for Neptune himself to use as a horn.**

Two of the following trails are located at the main refuge off the Sanibel-Captiva Road, the island's main thoroughfare. The third walk in the Bailey Tract is away from the main refuge, a few short miles away on Tarpon Bay Road. Time your hike on the main refuge to coincide with low tide, when the greatest abundance of birds will be present. The tide charts are in the local paper.

Nearest town: Sanibel
Start: At the main refuge or the separate Bailey Tract
Distance: Under 0.5 mile to almost 5 miles
Approximate hiking time: 3 hours total for all hikes
Difficulty: Easy
Trail surface: Natural, paved surface
Seasons: Best walking weather is in winter, when birding is also best.
Other trail users: Auto traffic on the Wildlife Drive shoulder; birders
Canine compatibility: No pets
Land status: National wildlife refuge

Fees and permits: Wildlife Drive entrance fee $5 per vehicle
Schedule: The Wildlife Drive is closed Friday, open Saturday to Thursday from 7:30 a.m. until 30 minutes before sunset. The education center opens at 9:00 a.m. daily with seasonal closings: at 5:00 p.m. January 1 through April 30 and at 4:00 p.m. the rest of the year. The refuge is most heavily visited during winter months.
Maps: Available at the visitor center
Trail contact: J.N. Ding Darling National Wildlife Refuge, 1 Wildlife Drive, Sanibel, FL 33957; (239) 472-1100; www.fws.gov/dingdarling

More Information

Local Information

Sanibel-Captiva Chamber of Commerce: www.sanibel-captiva.org.

Local Events/Attractions

Cyclists can use the Wildlife Drive and most of the trails as long as they obey the one-way rule of the road. From the Education Center, it is an 8-mile loop along Wildlife Drive returning along the main bike path along Sanibel-Captiva Road or a 4.8-mile loop along Wildlife Drive returning along the Indigo Trail.

The refuge's concessionaire, Tarpon Bay Explorers, conducts guided **tram tours** along the Wildlife Drive leaving from the Education Center parking lot. At the Tarpon Bay Recreation Area, Tarpon Bay Explorers provide **kayak/canoe and sea life interpretive tours** along with rental bicycles, kayaks, canoes, pontoon boats, and fishing equipment. They also offer fishing charters; (239) 472-8900 or www.tarponbayexplorers.com.

Ding Darling Days is held each October: www.dingdarlingdays.com.

In addition, **bike paths** extend for more than 20 miles on Sanibel, winding beside the main thoroughfare from the southern to northern tip.

Lodging

You'll find an extensive array of resorts and rental condos on Sanibel and Captiva Islands; www.fortmyers-sanibel.com.

Camping

Sites for tents or RVs are available at Periwinkle Trailer Park & Campground, 1119 Periwinkle Way, Sanibel Island, FL 33957; (239) 472-1433 or www.sanibelcamping.com.

Organizations

U.S. Fish & Wildlife Service: www.fws.gov.
Ding Darling Wildlife Society: www.dingdarlingsociety.org/dd_about.html.
J. N. "Ding" Darling Foundation: www.dingdarling.org.

22 Indigo Trail

The raccoons at Ding Darling NWR make a feast of the berries of the cabbage palm or sabal palm, Florida's state tree.

Start: Education center parking lot

Distance: 4.8-mile loop

Approximate hiking time: 2.5 hours

Finding the trailhead: The refuge is located 15 miles southwest of Fort Myers on Sanibel Island, off the main Sanibel-Captiva Road. The Indigo Trail starts from the most accessible place of all, the Education Center parking lot. **GPS:** N26 26.750' W082 06.774'

The Hike

The trail quickly moves onto a boardwalk that goes through a tropical hammock and then a mangrove forest. Once you cross the Wildlife Drive, you'll start a shell path that

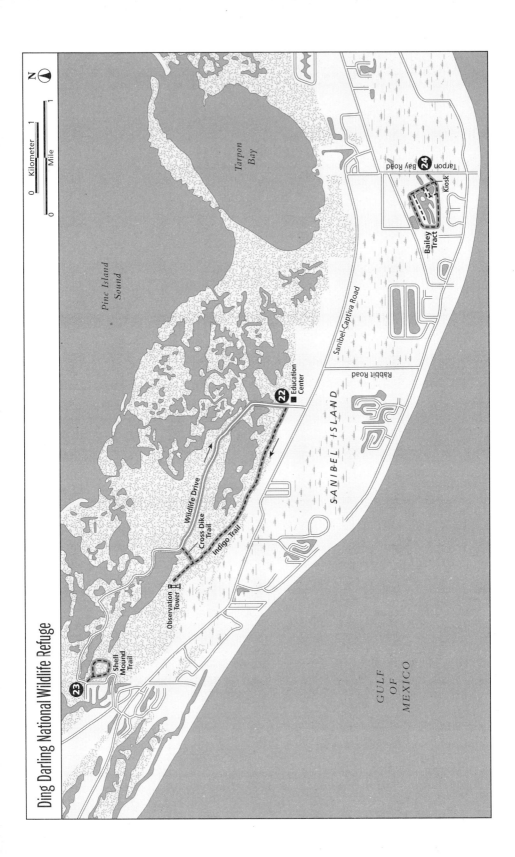

Ding Darling National Wildlife Refuge

will be in open sun except in early morning. The trail follows the top of a mosquito impoundment. According to legend, Sanibel was the worst place for mosquitoes in the lower United States with 365,000 of the blood suckers caught in just a single night in a single trap in the 1950s. It is not nearly as bad today, but need we say take bug spray?

Unfortunately, the foliage blocks the water for the much of the initial walk, making it difficult to see the birds so common here. But pay attention to the mangrove roots and branches since there is always the opportunity to see birds that have decided to wander off the beaten path. Finally, after the first 1.5 miles the trail opens up on the right to reveal the waterway and the mudflats that have been so long hidden.

One bird in particular everyone hopes to see is the colorful pink roseate spoonbill, the emblematic bird of Florida. Almost extinct by the mid-twentieth century, it has rebounded strongly. The spoonbill's broad, flattened beak, whose tip is not too different from the shape of a manatee's tail, is characteristic of spoonbills both young and old. The bill is important in feeding, where the bird moves its bill from side to side underwater in search of shrimp and small fish. The flat bill also comes in handy for searching soft shallow muddy areas for insects and crustaceans.

Immature birds display a soft pink on their wings and back that darkens with age. They attain their bright pink, mature colors at about three years of age. The pink is accented by a distinctive orange tail and shoulders, rump, and chest patch that are all bright red. The skin on the sides and back of the neck is a dark black. A little gaudy overall, perhaps, like the dresses of French can-can girls, but it's no wonder plume hunters wanted these birds so badly they almost completely exterminated them.

Continue straight to the trail's end at an observation tower. Before turning around and retracing your steps, it's time for a decision. Do you want to take a different return and walk the Cross Dike Trail to the Wildlife Drive and the Education Center or go back the same way you came? If you have any interest in photography or bird watching, take the Cross Dike Trail and turn right to enjoy the open vistas of the Wildlife Drive as you walk to the trailhead. Ibis are common in this area but you never know what you might see, especially at low tide when birds of every type come in to feed.

Miles and Directions

0.0 Depart from the Education Center parking lot.

0.2 Cross Wildlife Drive.

0.7 Pass 0.5-mile marker, based on starting from Wildlife Drive.

1.5 Waterway opens.

1.8 Cross Dike Trail is on the right; go straight.

2.0 Reach observation tower; retrace steps.

2.2 Turn left onto Cross Dike Trail.

2.4 Reach Wildlife Drive; turn right.

4.6 Arrive back at entrance to Wildlife Drive.

4.8 Arrive back at parking lot.

23 Shell Mound Trail

The Shell Mound Trail passes over an old Calusa Indian shell mound.

See map on page 90.
Start: Parking area of Wildlife Drive

Distance: 0.4-mile loop
Approximate hiking time: 30 minutes

Finding the trailhead: From the Education Center, follow Wildlife Drive about 3 miles to the Shell Mound Trail. Or take Sanibel-Captiva Road northwest then turn right (north) onto Wildlife Drive to reach Shell Mound Trail. The trailhead is located on the left, near the end of the designated parking area on Wildlife Drive. **GPS:** N26 28.437' W082 09.144'

The Hike

This boardwalk trail loops through a hardwood hammock that's sustained considerable damage. In addition, some of the non-native species are being removed, so the landscape will be changing dramatically in the coming years.

This hammock, growing atop a Calusa Indian shell mound, offers many tall examples of gumbo limbo, sea grape, sable palms, and live oaks. The trees provide shelter for indigo snakes, diamondback rattlesnakes, and gopher tortoises. Best known for its peeling bark, the gumbo limbo has a green bark that turns red when it peels and new layers of bark emerge. You'll see several examples close-up since a number of the trees lean over the boardwalk, almost blocking the path.

The Calusa were not agriculturally oriented but looked to the sea for their survival. They were Sanibel's first serious shell collectors, employing a variety of shells to make their tools. For instance, whelk shells could be turned into an axe while oyster shells made ideal drinking cups. When the tools wore out, they were discarded to create shell mounds like this one.

Sanibel Island is world famous for its shelling. A huge horse conch like this one is a real prize.

24 Bailey Tract

See map on page 90.
Start: Bailey Tract parking area

Distance: 1.1-mile lollipop loop
Approximate hiking time: 40 minutes

Finding the trailhead: The Bailey Tract is located 2.2 miles from the main refuge. Leaving the refuge, turn left and drive southeasterly to the intersection with Tarpon Bay Road; turn right onto Tarpon Bay Road. Continue for about 0.7 mile until you see the pedestrian crossing sign. Entrance to the Bailey Tract will be on the right. **GPS:** N26 25.738' W082 04.826'

The Hike

The 100-acre tract protects a freshwater marsh containing a series of five hiking/biking trails that thoroughly explore the area. The trails are of varying length, from 0.25 mile to 1.1 miles. The following description covers the 1.1-mile perimeter Red Trail that provides easy access to all other paths.

From the Bailey Tract parking lot, take the common access trail to the kiosk with information about the habitat and the animals that live here. Then turn right to start the perimeter trail, which shares the path with the 1-mile Yellow Trail. You'll immediately pass Ant Pond on the left, which the 0.25-mile Orange Trail encircles. You'll soon come to the 0.35-mile Green Trail that circles both Ant Pond and a marshy section.

Before long the Yellow Trail will turn left to encircle the extensive Mangrove Head Pond. The Red Trail joins the Blue Trail, continuing straight ahead, then turns left and parallels a large marshy impoundment. Keep an eye out for alligators and the osprey that hunt here regularly. Next the Blue Trail turns off in a sharp left to continue beside the impoundment. Stay on the Red Trail til the Yellow Trail arrives from the left to continue with you for the rest of the hike as you explore the fringes of Mangrove Head Pond. One more sharp left and you're soon back at the information kiosk and the parking lot.

Miles and Directions

0.0 Start from parking area.

0.1 Arrive at information kiosk. Go right past Ant Pond.

0.2 Yellow Trail goes left, Blue Trail comes in from the left.

0.3 Turn left to border large impoundment.

0.5 Turn left again.

0.8 Final left turn, to border Mangrove Head Pond.

1.1 Return to kiosk. Go straight to parking lot.

Everglades National Park: Homestead to Flamingo Day Hikes

While it is possible to hike the 40-mile road from the visitor center at the main park entrance to Flamingo at the southern tip, few ever do it. If making the trek is your goal, do it only in the cooler weather of January and February. To overnight, you must camp everywhere. The inn at the end, Flamingo Lodge, is closed as this is written due to storm damage. Hopefully it will be rebuilt in a new vastly improved incarnation. The old Flamingo Lodge had its charm but the rooms were very outdated.

The presence of mosquitoes dominates Everglades activities, and with decades of experience behind them, the NPS rangers at Flamingo have developed a warning system you definitely should check out at the ranger station before hiking the area. It's their infamous Mosquito Meter, which uses a caricature of a female mosquito in which her proboscis (which she uses to suck blood) points to the day's condition, ranging from fair to "unbearable." It's low-tech but it gets the message across. Go prepared.

The following day hikes, all over 3 miles in length, are on the main park road or at Flamingo.

Nearest town: Florida City
Start: Most hikes start from Flamingo
Distance: 3 to 7 miles
Approximate hiking time: 2 to 5 hours, depending on trail
Difficulty: Easy to moderate
Trail surface: Natural surface
Seasons: December to March is best three ways: for cool weather, the fewest mosquitoes, and best wildlife viewing.
Other trail users: Cyclists, wildlife photographers, birders
Canine compatibility: No pets
Land status: National park
Fees and permits: Entrance fee $10 per vehicle, good for 7 days at Homestead and Shark Valley entrances
Schedule: Homestead's main park road is open 24 hours a day (thanks to anglers who launch and return at all hours). Flamingo visitor center hours are seasonal.
Maps: Ask at the visitor center or entrance station

Trail contacts: Everglades National Park, 40001 State Road 9336, Homestead, FL 33034; (305) 242-7700 or www.nps.gov/ever. Flamingo Visitor Center, (239) 695-2945 or www.nps.gov/ever/pphtml/facilities.html. This center is staffed fulltime only from November to April.
Special considerations: These longer trails do not receive much walking traffic compared to the short walks in the Everglades detailed in the Pinelands Short Loop hike description. Some pathways flood easily, so you might want to call ahead. Also, bicycles are allowed on many of these same trails. That's not really a compatible situation since trail sections are too narrow for multi-use but these days there seem to be more cyclists than hikers.

Mosquitoes in these sections can be particularly ferocious. Carry a mosquito head net unless you care to inhale some of the buggers. Head nets are sold in most Homestead/Florida City sporting goods departments and may be available at the Flamingo Marina.

More Information

Local Information
Greater Homestead/Florida City Chamber of Commerce: www.chamberinaction.com.

Lodging
Florida City: Flamingo Lodge is closed.

Camping
Accommodations are divided into two different categories. Frontcountry camping for tents and RVs is available at one of the two developed campgrounds, Long Pine Key and Flamingo. Camping at Long Pine Key is on a first-come basis: 800-365-CAMP or http://reservations.nps.gov. Camping is free during the wet season (if you can stand not only the damp ground but the hordes of mosquitoes).

Backcountry camping is available on ground and beach sites, though most backcountry sites are on elevated *chickees* and can be reached only by boat. Contact www.nps.gov/ever/planyour visit/backcamp.htm.

Organizations
The South Florida National Parks Trust: www.southfloridaparks.org.
National Park Service: www.nps.gov.

25 Pinelands Long Loop

The morning glory flower opens in the morning for pollination by hummingbirds, butterflies, bees, and other daytime insects. The flower typically lasts for only one morning, dying in the afternoon. New flowers bloom each day.

Start: Pinelands Walking Trail parking lot
Distance: 5.9-mile loop

Approximate hiking time: 3.5 hours

Finding the trailhead: On the main park road to Flamingo, just past the road to Long Pine Key Campground, look for Gate G11 on the right (north) of the main park road. The gate is located 0.8 mile south of the turnoff to the Pinelands Short Loop Trail, and the campground is 2.3 miles north of the turnoff to Royal Palm Hammock trails, Anhinga and Gumbo Limbo. **GPS:** N26 26.750' W082 06.774'

The Hike

As on the shorter Pinelands Short Loop Trail, you're entering one of Florida's rarest habitats, with a far more extensive look of the pine rocklands characterized by Dade County slash pine and limestone karst formations. The trees you see today were pruned (another way of saying they were snapped like matchsticks) by Hurricane Andrew in 1992. It will be decades before the forest fully recovers, but there's also something to be said for a more open area that allows the sunlight to illuminate the trail. Unsightly as the fallen trees may seem—they are increasingly less prominent in the landscape as new growth takes over—this is part of the natural cycle.

We humans tend to judge our surroundings based on our own limited life spans, irrelevant in the scheme of things. Seventy or a hundred years is insignificant compared to how the world works. Florida once was immersed with as much as 20 to 30 feet of ocean for millions of years, hence the state's limestone base. Then the sea fell as much as 300 feet before rising again to its present levels an estimated 6,000 years ago. The rocklands here are full of holes and fissures and, true to their undersea beginnings, they act as a sponge, soaking up acidic rainfall and decaying plant matter that continually reshapes them.

As a result, the hiking path here is uneven and requires constant attention to keep from twisting an ankle in small depressions that are actually large solution holes in the making. (Bowl-shaped depressions in the limestone bedrock caused by erosion, the beginnings of a sinkhole where water levels are high and the limestone crust thin.) You'll pass some large ones, too—some as large as an automobile, filled with water and stuff that looks like primordial soup. The brownish goop is called periphyton, a mix of algae and fungi that feeds microscopic animals throughout the Everglades. A good place to see it in the dry season is on the first section of the Mahogany Hammock Boardwalk. Keep in mind that dried periphyton is easy walking, like volcanic wash. But when it's wet, it's slippery, and it will put you on your butt.

Long Pine Key boasts a good network of connecting trails through this forest of slash pines. Residents include opossums, raccoons, white-tailed deer, and even the endangered Florida panther. The best chance for seeing them is not to retrace your footsteps on the 3.8-mile linear hike, but to turn it into an out-and-back round-trip walk of 7.6 miles (four and a half hours).

Or consider turning the walk into a loop by using the main park road as a connector trail. Then your walk is reduced to 5.9 miles (three and a half hours) and you still need only a single vehicle. With a single car, park in the Pinelands Short Loop Trail parking lot to reduce the amount of time spent on the main park road at a single stretch. Also, this arrangement will provide a restroom stop at each end of the hike. Starting from the Pinelands Trail parking lot, walk south along the main park road to Gate G11, on your left.

Beginning and ending the walk via the main park road will sometimes reveal remarkable wildlife sightings. I've seen a bobcat on the side of the main road and an alligator walking between lakes. And mosquitoes are fewer along the main park road.

With two vehicles, park the second one at the northernmost gate, G9, but do not start there since it tends to be wet. Park the first car at Gate G11. This reduces the hike sharply, down to 3.8 miles and about two and a half hours.

Miles and Directions

0.0 Start from Pinelands Trail parking lot; go left on main park road.

0.8 Arrive at Gate G11; go left.

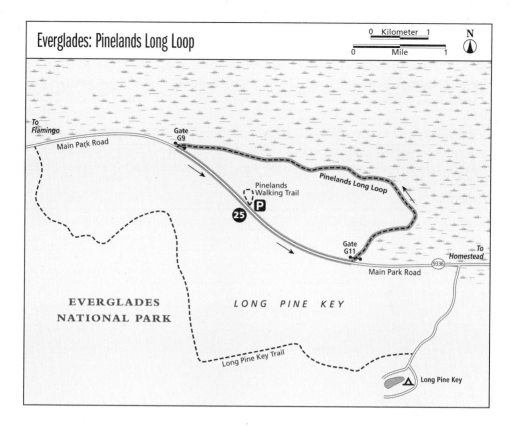

Everglades: Pinelands Long Loop

1.6 Trail curves left.

2.0 Pass by large solution holes.

2.3 Bear left at mudflat.

2.9 Trail passes through small hammock.

3.3 Pass another large solution hole.

4.0 Trail becomes slippery as it moves away from prairie.

4.3 Walk through low area.

4.6 Walk around Gate G9. Turn left to walk on shoulder of Main Park Road.

5.9 Walks ends at Pinelands parking lot.

26 Snake Bight/Rowdy Bend Trails

Start: Snake Bight trailhead
Distance: 7.3-mile loop

Approximate hiking time: 4 hours

Finding the trailhead: From Homestead follow the Main Park Road toward Flamingo for 43.4 miles. The Snake Bight trailhead is on the south side of the road, 5.4 miles north of Flamingo. The Rowdy Bend trailhead is 2.7 miles closer to Flamingo. **GPS:** N25 12.667' W080 52.479'

The Hikes

The main attraction of both trails is the chance to see wild flamingoes at Florida Bay. The Flamingo area itself is named after the colorful birds that, due to overhunting, disappeared from the Everglades for decades. Apparently flamingoes never did breed in Florida, though birds from Cuba and the Bahamas traveled here in large numbers until 1902.

In recent years small numbers of Florida's famous pink bird have been spotted in Florida Bay at the end of the 1.7-mile (one way) Snake Bight Trail. Even if the flamingoes are not present, you still have the opportunity for good bird watching at an observation deck overlooking the water. The Rowdy Bend Trail, extending 2.6 miles one way, joins the Snake Bight Trail after following an old roadbed shaded by buttonwoods, then meandering through open coastal prairie. It offers another chance to look for flamingoes on Florida Bay.

Although most people hike the trails individually, we suggest combining both trails to turn them into a 7.3-mile loop trail, with a 2.7-mile connecting trail along Main Park Road. This extended route includes passing Mrazek Pond, one of the most famous places in the Everglades for photographing birds when conditions are right, and Coot Bay Pond. Obviously, a camera is as important as mosquito protection. Two vehicles, one at each trailhead, would shorten this walk to 4.6 miles.

Mosquitoes have always been a serious problem around Flamingo. A visitor in 1893 recorded that the village on stilts consisted of thirty-eight shacks where he saw an oil lamp put out by a fog of mosquitoes. Smudge pots were the only defense, and all the buildings were covered with soot.

Today we're more high tech, using full mosquito protection that includes a head net. Snake Bight Trail should probably be renamed Mosquito Bite Trail. Snake Bight refers to a channel on Florida Bay, not to any extreme reptile dangers along the pathway; though it's always prudent to be watchful and prepared.

Miles and Directions

0.0 Begin at Snake Bight trailhead, 5.4 miles north of Flamingo Visitor Center.

0.7 Go straight; pass old bridge to unused Crocodile Point trail system.

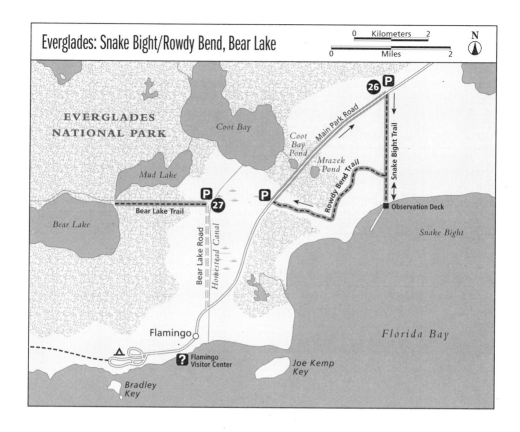

Everglades: Snake Bight/Rowdy Bend, Bear Lake

1.4 Rowdy Bend Trail comes in from the right.

1.7 Arrive at Florida Bay observation platform; retrace footsteps.

2.0 Turn left onto Rowdy Bend Trail.

2.5 Trail enters dark tropical forest.

3.5 Pass old trail marker; trail turns right.

4.6 Reach Main Park Road; turn right to walk on shoulder.

7.3 Reach Snake Bight trailhead.

27 Bear Lake Trail

The osprey, a fish hawk often mistaken for the bald eagle, is found in Florida almost everywhere there is water.

See map on page 101.
Start: Snake Bight trailhead

Distance: 3.5 miles out and back
Approximate hiking time: 2–3 hours

Finding the trailhead: Follow Bear Lake Road, located about 0.5 mile north of the Flamingo visitor center, north from Main Park Road to the Bear Lake Trail parking area. If Bear Lake Road is closed due to heavy rains, park on the side of the Main Park Road, but do not block the entrance. Then trudge 1.75 miles along the road to the official trailhead. If you start from the main road, the hike's round-trip distance is 7 miles (three to four hours). **GPS:** N25 08.938' W080 55.389'

The Hike

Whether you drive or walk the Bear Lake access road, you'll parallel the Homestead Canal, which was dredged to create a channel from Flamingo to Coot Bay. The limestone pulled out of the ground to make the waterway became the roadbed for Bear Lake Road. The canal is used today by paddlers and tour boats as well as those adventurous souls wanting to paddle the 100-mile long Wilderness Waterway, camping in Seminole-style chickees and rare dry ground along the route. Paddling the Wilderness Waterway is probably the single greatest adventure you can make in Florida since you have to be totally self-sufficient for at least a week.

The most memorable part of my Wilderness Waterway trip took place in the Homestead Canal, on the final night, as two of us were pushing hard to get to Flamingo before dark. But it was already twilight as we proceeded through the canal, making it hard to see anything in the water. Suddenly our canoe encountered a sunken object just below the surface: an alligator. Imagine the surprise of all three parties, and the terrible feeling of the two humans now resting on the gator's back. The reptile began thrashing wildly while we held onto the sides of the canoe, praying we would not tip. The sound of a gator whipping itself against fiberglass is an unusual one I hope never to hear again. Finally the gator sank underwater and disappeared—our signal to depart. As furiously as we paddled for the next half mile, we could have towed a water skier.

▶ Protecting over 1.5 million acres, Everglades National Park is the third largest national park in the lower forty-eight states, behind Yellowstone National Park (number 2) and Death Valley National Park (number 1).

You shouldn't encounter anything as exciting along the canal on your way to the Bear Lake trailhead. The designated trail, 1.8 miles each way, is rich in both bird and plant life. First, the trail passes through a dense hardwood hammock mixed with mangroves and thirty other different tree species, an excellent spot for woodland birds.

The trail follows the old Homestead Canal, built in 1922, which provides access to Bear Lake, your destination. At several points along the way, and especially near the end, the mangroves crowd the trail and form a fairly thick canopy. The hike ends at a small marl beach on Bear Lake. If you're in luck, the trees will be filled with white egrets. And in the water? Alligators, what else? Then, it's time to retrace your steps.

Miles and Directions

0.0 Start from the trailhead on the left.

0.6 Mangroves crowd trail; continue.

1.6 Arrive at Bear Lake.

1.8 Trail ends at small beach; retrace steps.

3.5 Arrive back at trailhead and parking lot.

Long Haulers

28 Jonathan Dickinson State Park: East Loop Trail

The anhinga, also known as the water turkey or snake bird, must dry out between its dives for fish since it has poorly developed oil glands, so its feathers aren't as waterproof as those of other water birds.

This 11,500-acre park is named for Jonathan Dickinson, who in 1696 was ship-wrecked about 5 miles from here. Dickinson was probably one of the first Europeans to sample palmetto berries, a staple of the local Jaegas Indians diet. He reported, "They taste like rotten cheese steeped in tobacco juice." Obviously the berries are an acquired taste.

◀ *The sabal palm, aka sabal palmetto and cabbage palm, is Florida's state tree.*

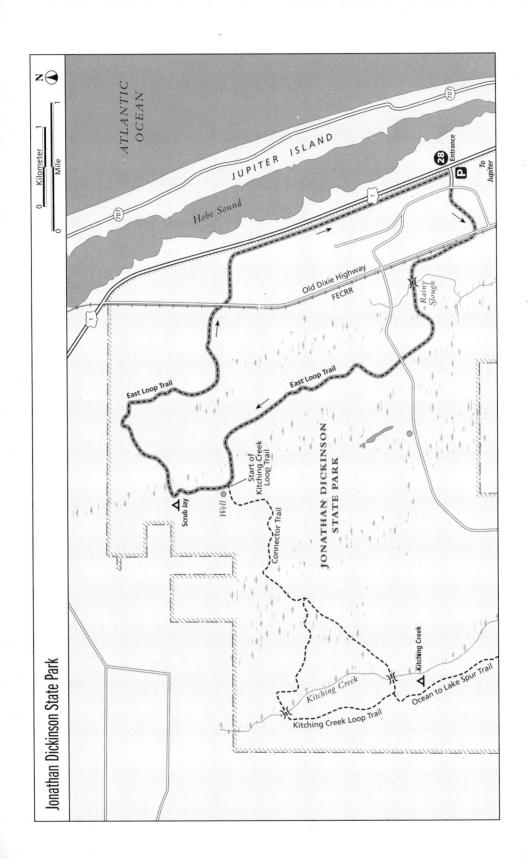

Jonathan Dickinson State Park

The trail system here features a series of loops. Despite nearby development, more than 500 animal species (including bald eagles, scrub jays, and gopher tortoises) live within the park. About 20 percent of the park is covered in coastal sand pine scrub, a habitat so rare it is designated "globally imperiled."

Nearest towns: Hobe Sound, Jupiter
Start: North end of main parking lot
Distance: 9.8-mile loop
Approximate hiking time: 8 to 9 hours
Difficulty: Easy
Trail surface: Natural, paved, and boardwalk
Seasons: Fall through early spring
Other trail users: Hikers only
Canine compatibility: Leashed pets permitted on most trails; pets prohibited in cabins, at primitive campsites, and on backpacking trails.
Land status: State park
Fees and permits: Park admission fee under $5
Schedule: Open 8:00 a.m. to sunset
Maps: Available at the ranger station
Trail contact: Jonathan Dickinson State Park, 16450 Southeast Federal Highway, Hobe Sound, FL 33455; (772) 546-2771; www .floridastateparks.org/jonathandickinson

Finding the trailhead: From Jupiter, travel 3.5 miles north on U.S. Highway 1; the park entrance is on the left. The trailhead is located at the north end of the park's main parking lot. **GPS:** N27 00.246' W080 06.087'

The Hike

This trail follows a varied path, first going through sand pine scrub, then across Old Dixie Highway (old US 1), and into stands of live oak. The Scrub Jay campsite is about 5 miles in, including the side trail to the site. (*Note:* Camp within the circle of trees marked with white rings on their trunks, and use the fire ring for ground fires.)

After going northeast for a mile, the trail then goes south for the next few miles, through pine and palmetto and across a fire road. The trail parallels and crosses tracks of the Cross Florida East Coast Railroad before returning to the park gate.

Miles and Directions

0.0 Start at the north end of the parking lot near the park entrance.
0.1 Cross the main entrance road.
0.3 Reach an unnamed lake.
0.6 Cross old railroad tracks.
1.4 Cross a footbridge.
2.3 Cross the park road.
4.3 Pass the junction of East Loop with the connector to the Kitching Creek Loop Trail (see option below). Bear right to stay on East Loop.
4.7 Pass a side trail to Scrub Jay campsite.
5.2 Cross a wooden bridge.
7.3 Cross old US 1 and railroad tracks.
8.4 Cross a paved road.
9.8 Arrive back at the parking lot.

OCEAN TO LAKE SPUR TRAIL

Jonathan Dickinson State Park is an important link in Florida's newest long-distance hike, the 70-mile-long Ocean to Lake Spur Trail, now almost complete. The ambitious walk begins just south of Jonathan Dickinson at Hobe Sound on the Atlantic coast; it ends at the Port Mayaca Recreation Area on the shores of massive Lake Okeechobee. Although a complete route has been mapped out, several small sections still need land management approval before the walk is open to the public.

The proposed track starts at Hobe Sound Beach at the end of Bridge Road, goes up Old A1A, and then enters Jonathan Dickinson State Park, where the trail becomes mostly natural footpath. From Jonathan Dickinson, the hike meanders through Jupiter's Riverbend Park and the Loxahatchee Slough Natural Area before connecting with the existing Florida Trail on the J. W. Corbett Wildlife Management Area (see Florida Trail Segment hike). From Corbett, the walk heads northwest into the DuPuis Management Area (see Loop Trails). On the western side of DuPuis' Loop 3, the path turns sharply west to arrive at Lake Okeechobee, passing through sugar-cane fields on the way.

Once the trail is completed, hikers will need only a single permit for the entire trail. Until then, hikers must obtain a permit from each land management agency. The Florida Trail Association, which laid out the trail, sponsors three-day walks along the route; check their Web site at www.floridatrail.org. Look under "planned activities."

Option: The 4.2-mile Kitching Creek Loop is an extension of the East Loop. It adds about six hours to the East Loop Trail, but it's best to make the entire hike an overnighter. It passes through low pine flatwoods and along Kitching Creek, a tributary of the Loxahatchee River. Initially the trail penetrates thick saw palmetto and South Florida slash pine, part of a once-continuous forest of century-old virgin pines more than 90 feet tall and 2 feet in diameter. Settlers cut most of the trees to make homes from the hard, termite-resistant wood.

▶ **The Loxahatchee River was Florida's first federally designated Wild and Scenic River.**

Kitching Creek itself is a cypress strand—a long, narrow band of trees following a natural watercourse. The area was logged in the 1940s. The creek is named for the Kitching family, who bought the land from the state of Florida for $1.25 an acre in 1886. The woman who purchased the land lived in England and probably never actually saw the property, or Florida, for that matter.

As you walk here, look for cabbage palm (also called sabal palm or sabal palmetto), the official Florida state tree. Similar in appearance to the saw palmetto when young, the cabbage palm is used to make "swamp cabbage" by cutting out the heart of the tree, which kills it. Swamp cabbage is found on many rural menus.

Although Indians ate the berries of the saw palmetto, don't try the black berries of the gallberry, a member of the holly family, whose leaves have a few teeth on each side of the leaves. Gallberries are poisonous. Saw palmetto is rarely harmed by fire because its roots are well protected underground. Settlers prized the bushes as material for making yard brooms.

This optional section of trail begins at the junction of the connector trail and East Loop, 4.3 miles along East Loop Trail. Turn westward at the well, walking about 1.5 miles along the connector to the Kitching Creek Loop Trail. Take the left fork to walk the loop clockwise. At about 6.6 miles, cross the creek via a footbridge. About 0.2 mile later, pass a blue-blazed side trail that leads 0.5 mile to a camping area—unless you want to spend the night there. At 7.8 miles, cross another footbridge over the creek. About a mile later, meet the connector trail and walk northeast back toward East Loop. At the junction with East Loop you may choose to return the way you came (4.3 miles) or head north then east and south along US 1 to complete the loop (5.5 miles).

More Information

Local Information
Stuart/Martin County Chamber of Commerce: www.goodnature.org.

Local Events/Attractions
A local character of note was "The Wild Man of the Loxahatchee," a trapper named Nelson, who died in 1968. Nelson had built a popular wildlife zoo near his home, which the state took over after his death. The **Trapper Nelson Interpretive Site** is upriver from the state park. Visitors can reach Trapper Nelson's **zoo** by taking the thirty-passenger *Loxahatchee Queen* from the park. The two-hour boat trip is available Wednesday through Sunday.

    Canoe rentals are available for exploring the shores of the Loxahatchee River.

Lodging
The park has twelve rental cabins near the Loxahatchee River. Cabins include everything but sheets and towels. Call (561) 746-1466 for information and reservations.

Camping
There are two campgrounds within the park with 135 sites in addition to primitive camping on the Florida Trail at Miles 5 and 9. Reservations: (800) 326-3521; www.reserveamerica.com/index.jsp.

Organizations
Florida Department of Environmental Protection/Division of Recreation and Parks: www.dep .state.fl.us/parks.

29 J. W. Corbett Wildlife Management Area: Florida Trail Segment

Adjacent to the DuPuis Management Area, the J. W. Corbett Wildlife Management Area is home to a wide array of wildlife, including red-cockaded woodpeckers, bald eagles, deer, and wild hogs. In spring and summer, wildflowers transform the landscape with dramatic color. This is wilderness hiking where you may need to wade low areas after heavy rains. Carry plenty of water; none is available along the trail or at the campsites.

▶ **About a dozen pair of sandhill cranes winter at J. W. Corbett Wildlife Management Area.**

This 14-mile section of the Florida National Scenic Trail (FNST) within the management area passes through classic pine flatwoods and saw palmetto. It's also a segment of the Ocean to Lake Spur Trail, which runs from the Atlantic Ocean to Lake Okeechobee. This is a public hunting area—heed "Special considerations" below. Also in this management area, the Hungryland Boardwalk and Trail (described in Short Family Walks) is great for families with small children.

Nearest town: Indiantown
Start: Everglades Youth Conservation Camp
Distance: 28.0 miles out and back
Approximate hiking time: Overnight hike
Difficulty: Easy to moderate
Trail surface: Natural surface, boardwalk
Seasons: Fall through early spring; a public hunting area September to April
Other trail users: Equestrians, cyclists on Florida Trail
Canine compatibility: Leashed pets permitted
Land status: Wildlife management area
Fees and permits: Daily use permit required (under $5), available at sporting goods stores and county tax offices

Schedule: Open daylight hours
Maps: Available on-site or from the Florida Trail Association (FTA)
Trail contact: The Florida Fish and Wildlife Conservation Commission: (561) 625-5122; www.myfwc.com/recreation/jw_corbett
Special considerations: This is a public hunting area. During hunts, hikers should wear 500 square inches of blaze-orange clothing above the waist, and it must be visible in both front and back. Hunting schedule is available at www.myfwc.com/hunting.

Finding the trailhead: From Interstate 95 in West Palm Beach, take the Northlake Boulevard exit. Drive west about approximately 12.3 miles, crossing the Beeline Expressway (State Road 710). Take a right onto Seminole Pratt Whitney Road. The J. W. Corbett Wildlife Management Area entrance is just ahead. The trailhead is at the Everglades Youth Camp on Stumper's Grade Road. **GPS:** N26 51.345' W080 18.163'

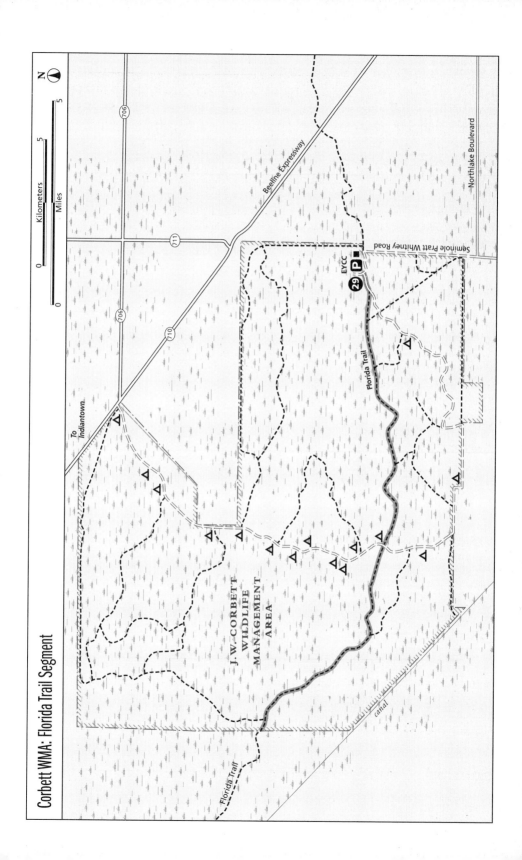

Corbett WMA: Florida Trail Segment

The Hike

The Florida Trail crosses wet prairie (prime wildflower territory) almost immediately. After crossing both improved and unimproved roads, look for a side trail to the first campsite, about 3 miles in.

The second campsite is at Mile 11, shortly after the trail crosses an unimproved road. Near the end of the hike, the trail passes an electrical transmission line loaded with a half-million volts. The trail ends at the boundary between the Corbett Wildlife Management Area and the DuPuis Management Area. At this point you must retrace your steps, since there is no access for a vehicle to pick you up.

Miles and Directions

0.0   Start at Everglades Youth Conservation Camp trailhead.

0.9   Cross a wet prairie.

1.2   Cross a power line right-of-way.

5.0   Pass side trail to camping area.

7.0   Pass through a cypress meadow area.

9.0   Cross a canal.

11.0   Reach Little Gopher camping area.

11.3   Cross a canal.

11.8   Cross a power line right-of-way.

14.0   Reach the wildlife management area boundary, your turnaround point. Retrace your route.

28.0   Arrive back at the youth camp and trailhead.

More Information

Local Information
Palm Beach County Convention and Visitors Bureau: www.palmbeachfl.com.

Lodging
Lodging is available at Indiantown (10 miles north), West Palm Beach (25 miles southeast), and Jupiter (15 miles east).

Camping
There are two primitive campsites on the Florida Trail, at Miles 5 and 11. A permit is required to stay overnight at the campsites, and fires can be built only in designated areas.

Organizations
Florida Fish and Wildlife Conservation Commission: www.myfwc.com/recreation/jw_corbett.

The **Friends of Corbett** meet monthly to plan activities and hold an annual barbecue; P.O. Box 16309, West Palm Beach, FL 33416-6309.

30 DuPuis Management Area: Loop Trails

Alligators are normally passive around humans, but every once in a while you find one that appears to regard you as lunch—which is why they always deserve respect.

Located along the northeastern edge of the Everglades in Martin and Palm Beach Counties, much of this 21,900-acre area was drained for pastureland and used to raise Dutch white-belted cattle, sheep, and goats. DuPuis Management Area is owned by the South Florida Water Management District (SFWMD), which intends to restore these wetlands, and is managed in cooperation with the Florida Fish and Wildlife Conservation Commission.

A 15-mile section of the Florida National Scenic Trail (FNST), divided into four stacked loops, goes through the area, which contains many rare and endangered species, including the Florida panther. This is a segment of the Ocean to Lake Spur Trail, another part of the FNST, running from the Atlantic Ocean to Lake Okeechobee. DuPuis is a public hunting area, and the trail is closed to hikers during scheduled hunts.

Nearest town: Port Mayaca
Start: Trailhead off State Road 76
Distance: 15.3-mile loop
Approximate hiking time: Overnight hike

Difficulty: Easy to moderate; may be wet for long stretches
Trail surface: Mostly natural surface
Seasons: Fall through early spring; closed

during hunting season except to through hikers. For hunting schedule, log on to www.myfwc.com/hunting.

Other trail users: Equestrian trails frequently crossed by hiking trail

Canine compatibility: Pets prohibited

Land status: Wildlife management area

Fees and permits: Daily use fee under $5

Schedule: Open daylight hours; visitor center at Gate 5 on SR 76

Maps: Available online at www.sfwmd.gov (click on Recreation, choose DuPuis Management Area, and click on Area Map) or from the Florida Trail Association (FTA)

Trail contacts: DuPuis Management Area, 23500 Southwest Kanner Highway, Canal Point, FL 33438; (561) 924-5310. The Florida Fish and Wildlife Conservation Commission regulates public access to the land: (407) 683-0748; www.myfwc.com/recreation. South Florida Water Management District: www.sfwmd.gov/site/index.php

Special considerations: This is a public hunting area. During hunts, hikers should wear 500 square inches of blaze-orange clothing above the waist, and it must be visible in both front and back. Hunting schedule is available at www.myfwc.com/hunting.

Finding the trailhead: Take SR 76 west from Interstate 95 or the Florida Turnpike near Stuart. Go 6 miles beyond its junction with State Road 710 at Indiantown. The signed trailhead is on the south side of SR 76 at Entrance Gate 2. **GPS:** N27 0.226' W080 19.813'

The Hike

Seminole Indians used the region as a sanctuary during the Seminole Indian War of 1835. However, surviving off the land was difficult. Hundreds of starving Seminoles were captured and sent to Oklahoma. This region then became known as the "Hungryland," a term still used in some places today.

Entrance Gate 2, about 1 mile west of Gate 1, is the entrance to the hiking trail. The Florida Trail Association, in cooperation with the water management district, has developed a network of 22 miles of hiking trails. The trails are part of the Florida Trail system and are arranged to provide hikes of various lengths. There are four stacked loop trails that range from 5 miles in length to nearly 16 miles, and a 7-mile extension from the last loop that connects to the J. W. Corbett Wildlife Management Area hiking trail.

▶ **A partially covered fishing pier is available at the northern end of the DuPuis Management Area.**

The Florida Trail Association provides all trail maintenance. Rectangular orange blazes on trees and posts mark the main hiking routes. Blue blazes mark side trails. Two blazes generally designate an abrupt change in direction. Carefully locate the next blaze before continuing. Remember to carry adequate water with you. A quiet hiker might see deer, wild turkeys, and bobcats.

If you would rather take a shorter hike and picnic, you may want to pack a sandwich and drink and take a 2-mile round-trip walk from Gate 2 to the old Governor's House. The house, which no longer is in use, is a small structure the previous owners used as a hunting camp. Today, there are several picnic tables under cover immediately next to the house and a charming old hand-pump well that your children will enjoy

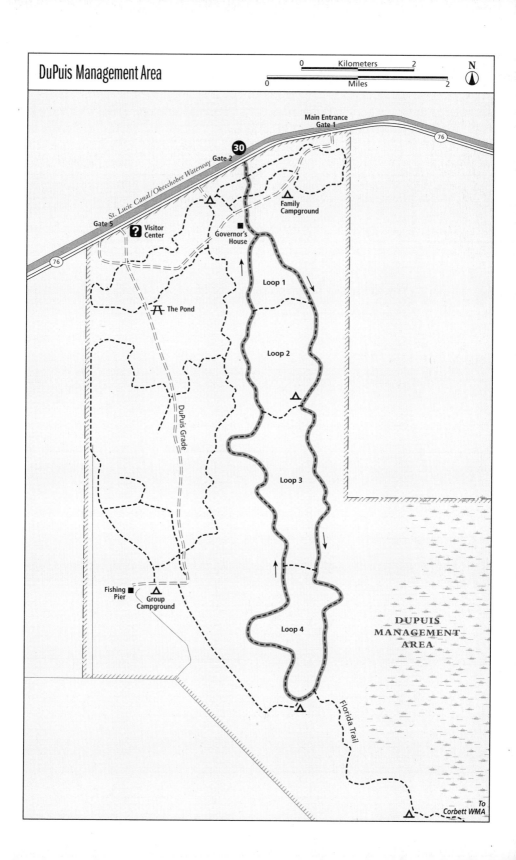

DuPuis Management Area

Kilometers
0   2

Miles
0   2

N

Main Entrance
Gate 1

76

30
Gate 2

St. Lucie Canal / Okeechobee Waterway

Family
Campground

Gate 5
Visitor
Center
?

Governor's
House

76

Loop 1

The Pond

Loop 2

DuPuis Grade

Loop 3

Fishing
Pier
Group
Campground

Loop 4

DUPUIS
MANAGEMENT
AREA

Florida Trail

To
Corbett WMA

(but don't drink the water—it isn't safe). The Governor's House is less than a mile from the trailhead at Gate 2.

Three primitive campsites are located along the hiking trail. The first is located on the east side of Loop 2; the second is at the south end of Loop 4; and the third is about 3 miles into the Corbett Trail at the south end of DuPuis.

This 15.3-mile walk meanders through an impressive array of landscapes that include pine flatwoods, ponds, cypress domes, wet prairies, and cabbage palm hammocks. About two-thirds of DuPuis is pinelands; the rest is cypress swamp and freshwater marsh. In the rainy season, portions of the roads are flooded.

The featured hike takes all four loops; using just the first two loops dramatically shortens the walk.

Just under a mile into the walk is the junction for the loops designated "East" and "West." Going eastward you'll pass several horse trails and a fence before coming to the first east-west link, about 2 miles from the trailhead. The junction for the second cross trail is just over 3 miles into the walk after crossing a fence. Another chance to loop from east to west is at about 5.5 miles.

If you follow the trail to Mile 7.7, the path makes its final loop to the west for the return trip. Overnighters can continue a short distance to the trail campsite.

Since this is a multiuse area open to trail rides, expect to cross a number of horse trails, as well as ditches and fences. They occur as often as one almost every half mile. As a result, unlike in other forests, where it is possible to go for miles without finding a trace of another person, hikers in DuPuis are constantly reminded of people, places, and things.

Miles and Directions

0.0 Start at trailhead off SR 76.

0.6 Pass a side trail to Governor's House.

0.7 The access trail intersects Loop 1; bear left.

0.8 Cross a series of horse trails.

1.9 Reach the Loop 1 cross trail; go straight to begin Loop 2.

3.1 Pass a campsite on Loop 2.

3.2 Pass the Loop 2 cross trail, going straight to begin Loop 3.

4.6 Pass Boot Lake.

5.5 Pass the Loop 3 cross trail, going straight to begin Loop 4.

7.2 Reach the southern end of the DuPuis trail and the junction with the 6.8-mile connector trail to Corbett Wildlife Management Area.

7.7 Reach Loop 4 campsite.

9.6 Join the far west section of the Loop 3 trail; continue straight.

12.3 End Loop 3 and begin Loop 2.

13.5 End Loop 2 and begin Loop 1.

15.3 Arrive back at the SR 76 trailhead.

More Information

Local Information

Stuart/Martin County Chamber of Commerce: www.goodnature.org.
Palm Beach County Convention and Visitors Bureau: www.palmbeachfl.com.

Lodging

Lodging is available in Port Mayaca.

Camping

A permit is required to stay overnight at the primitive campsites. Contact the South Florida Water Management District: (561) 924-5310 or, in Florida only, (800) 432-2045.

Organizations

Florida Fish and Wildlife Conservation Commission, South Florida Water Management District: www.sfwmd.gov.

Walking the
Florida Keys

The forty-two islands that make up the Florida Keys curve 150 miles out into the Gulf of Mexico, arranged like carefully placed stepping stones dotting the water. The term "Keys" comes from the Spanish word *cayos,* meaning "little islands." Originally a haven for pirates, the Keys became the wrecking ground for Spanish treasure ships and home to British loyalists after the American Revolution.

Today, they are America's version of the Caribbean. Many Keys plants owe their origins to the Caribbean islands, their seeds carried here by wind or waves. Throughout the islands you'll find some of America's finest seascapes: the blue waters of the Atlantic to the east and south, the green seas of the Gulf of Mexico on the north and west. Because of all the emphasis on water sports, hiking is not normally associated with the Florida Keys. However, the state has provided a handful of unspoiled oases that provide a close-up look at this uncommonly striking landscape, and these can be accessed by foot.

The main road connecting the islands is known as both the Overseas Highway and U.S. Highway 1. This completely toll-free road contains bridges as short as 40 feet and as long as 7 miles and moves through lowlands surrounded on all sides by sea and sky. The roadway is lined with mile markers all the way, measuring the distance down to Mile Marker 1 in Key West. Mile markers are the landmarks everyone in the Keys uses for distance and directions.

The Keys are divided into three distinct regions. The Upper Keys extend from Key Largo to Lower Matecumbe. Key Largo is probably the most famous destination in the Keys, after Key West, thanks in part to the classic film *Key Largo* in which Humphrey Bogart and Lauren Bacall survived both Edward G. Robinson and a hurricane. The main landmark of the Middle Keys is the city of Marathon, while the Lower Keys extend from Big Pine Key to Key West.

WHERE ARE ALL THE BEACHES?

One of the biggest surprises—and disappointments—for first-time Keys visitors is the lack of beaches. Unlike the Panhandle with its beach walks that go for miles, sand beaches in the Keys are a rarity. Instead of soft sand, hard coral rock forms the majority of the shoreline. Those natural strands that do exist are often in state parks or tend to be man-made.

Where there is sand, it's often swathed in seaweed according to the season. Not pretty, but important since accumulated seaweed helps prevent the erosion of the existing sand. Further, the tangled mats filter out and trap sand stirred up by wave action, adding more sand to the beach. Finally, the seaweed provides fertilizer for plants that colonize and stabilize the shoreline.

◄ *Hermit crabs use abandoned shells for protection and must continually find larger ones as they grow.*

31 Dagny Johnson Key Largo Hammock Botanical State Park: Hammock Walk

The Key Largo Botanical State Park is part of a failed real estate development. The trail starts from the old entrance gate.

For most visitors, the Keys begin with their arrival in Key Largo via U.S. Highway 1. However, there is another way into the Keys via Card Sound Road, which will deliver you to this little known but ecologically important Dagny Johnson Key Largo Hammock Botanical State Park. Located on the site of a failed tourist resort, the 2,500-acre park contains the largest contiguous tract of subtropical West Indian hardwood hammock remaining in the United States. With more than eighty species, this small park contains a greater diversity of trees than some entire states.

A self-guided walk takes you past species rarely seen outside the Caribbean, including forty-four protected plants and animals such as the Schaus swallowtail butterfly and Key Largo wood rat. Most of the trail is an old surfaced road built for the resort, though short nature trails venture off-road and into the hammock.

Nearest town: Key Largo
Start: Parking lot on County Road 905
Distance: 1.11-mile lollipop loop
Approximate hiking time: 45 to 60 minutes

Difficulty: Easy
Trail surface: Hard surface on most of the walk; natural surface for nature trail
Seasons: Winter

Other trail users: Hikers only

Canine compatibility: Pets not allowed on beaches, in picnic shelters, or bathhouses. Leashed pets are permitted on nature trail.

Land status: State park .

Fees and permits: Entrance fee under $5

Schedule: Open 8:00 a.m. until sunset daily.

Maps: Available at the entrance

Trail contacts: Dagny Johnson Key Largo Hammock Botanical State Park, P.O. Box 487, Key Largo, FL 33037; (305) 451-1202 or www .floridastateparks.org/keylargohammock

Finding the trailhead: The entrance is located on CR 905 about a half mile north of where US 1 enters Key Largo. The alternate route into the Keys via Card Sound Road takes you right past the entrance. If you come into the Keys on US 1, be prepared to turn north (left) onto CR 905 almost as soon as you enter Key Largo. The parking area is in front of the archway intended for the Port Bougainvillea condo complex, which went bankrupt in 1985. **GPS:** N25 10.559' W080 22.172'

The Hike

The main trail is only a little over a mile long. To explore the backcountry, you'll need a permit, available at John Pennekamp Coral Reef State Park (see the next hike). Arrange for this permit in advance. It may not be possible to obtain one if you simply show up at Key Largo unannounced.

Although the park is best known for its tree and plant life, wildlife viewing here should not be ignored. Several tropical species reside here, including the white-crowned pigeon, mangrove cuckoo, and black-whiskered vireo. Migratory birds fly north through here in April, south in October. The park is also home to the rare American crocodile and the Key Largo wood rat. In the United States, the American crocodile is found only in saltwater areas of the Upper Keys and parts of the Everglades. A crocodile is easy to distinguish from an alligator by its pointed snout while alligators have blunt, rounded snouts and are blacker in color. Only an estimated 400 crocodiles survive in Florida.

▶ **The park is named for the late Dagny Johnson, a local environmental activist.**

The tropical hardwood hammock was not deliberately planted but was established by seeds brought here by wind, by waves, and in the digestive tracts of migratory birds. At one time, trees like these were dominant trees on many of the Florida Keys.

One of the more common trees is the poisonwood (Metopium toxiferum) or hog gum, related to poison sumac and poison oak. Like those more famous pests, poisonwood contains a sap that can cause a rash or blistering. The sap can be on any part of the tree, not just the leaves. The tree, which can grow to 40 feet high, is identified best by its brown wood color often streaked with red. The bark on older trees frequently peels like the harmless gumbo limbo, whose skin is entirely red. Ironically, poisonwood fruit is a favorite of many birds including the white-crowned pigeon.

You'll probably be surprised to come across native bamboo, very different from the large woody trees that were brought in from Asia. The Florida bamboo is simply a grass common throughout all South Florida. Furthermore, you'll encounter a native wild coffee plant with small seeds that resemble tiny coffee beans. Indeed, it was once used as a coffee substitute when the real item was scarce or unavailable. These days, its red fruit are enjoyed only by birds while its white flowers attract butterflies.

An extensive series of small metal interpretive signs line the main paved path, making it easy to identify unusual trees like the soldierwood, known for the loud "POP" its seed capsules make when it expels the seeds.

Going off-road on the nature trails, expect a lot of twisting and turning on these short trails. Pay attention to your landmarks or you could find yourself going the wrong way or needlessly repeating your steps.

Miles and Directions

0.00 Trailhead starts at cement archway with a chain to block motorized traffic.

0.10 Pass portable toilet.

0.14 Arrive at roundabout with picnic table. Go right. (Go left if you have a backcountry permit.)

0.27 Pass bench.

0.31 Turn left onto natural path to join nature trail. Pass stone wall.

0.34 Trail Ys. Go right.

0.41 Nature trail ends at park boundary. Go right to rejoin hardtop.

0.43 Trail Ts at bench. Go right.

0.51 Arrive back at nature trail path on the right. Go straight to return to entrance. Rejoin nature trail to explore more of the hammock.

0.53 Go left at bench.

0.56 Go left at junction. Trail ahead is a false one.

0.64 Go right to limestone quarry. Retrace steps to main trail and bear right.

0.69 Trail comes in from right. Go straight.

0.74 Turn right at stone wall.

0.76 Turn right to rejoin hardtop and retrace steps to trailhead.

1.11 Arrive back at parking lot.

More Information

Local Information

Monroe County Tourist Development Council: www.fla-keys.com/keylargo.

Key Largo Chamber of Commerce: www.keylargo.org.

Key West Citizen: www.keysnews.com.

Local Events/Attractions

Seasonal evening **lectures** are given Wednesday evenings from January through March. **Nature walks** are offered Thursday and Sunday mornings from October through March. Check the park Web site for current times and locations.

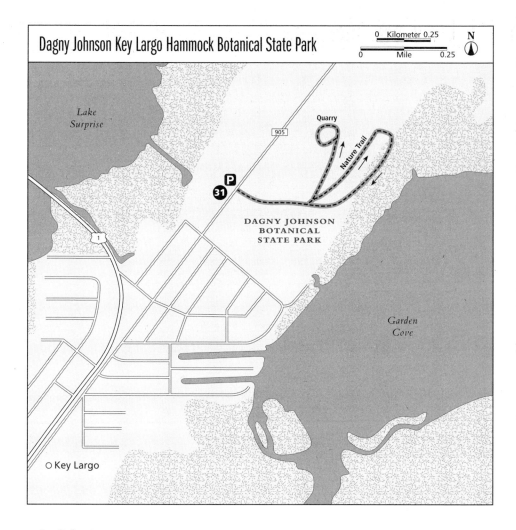

Lodging
Lodging is available in Key Largo.

Camping
Nearby, John Pennekamp Coral Reef State Park has sites for both tents and RVs.

Organizations
Florida Department of Environmental Protection/Division of Recreation and Parks: www.dep
.state.fl.us/parks.

32 John Pennekamp Coral Reef State Park: Mangrove and Wild Tamarind Trails

Best known for its scuba diving, John Pennekamp Coral Reef State Park also has two good short nature trails: one through the mangroves, the other inland.

The first underwater park in the United States, Pennekamp encompasses a huge area. It's 21 nautical miles long and 18 nautical miles wide, almost all of it below sea level. This has made Pennekamp the most popular location for snorkeling and scuba diving in the entire United States. The underwater vistas can be spectacular, with 650 species of colorful reef fish (such as neon-colored queen angels, grunts, snapper, and grouper) and more than 25 kinds of coral.

Few people visit Pennekamp to hike, yet the two short nature trails are definitely worth walking. One is a boardwalk trail through a mangrove forest, the other a self-guided nature trail winding through many tropical species with a good chance for seeing Liguus tree snails.

Nearest town: Key Largo
Start: Mile Marker 102.5
Distance: Two nature trails, each under 0.5 mile
Approximate hiking time: 1 hour for both trails

Difficulty: Easy
Trail surface: Boardwalk and natural surface
Seasons: Winter is the most enjoyable walking time. Summer weather is more appropriate for offshore snorkeling or scuba diving.

Other trail users: Hikers only
Canine compatibility: Pets in park must be leashed; not allowed on beaches, in picnic shelters, or bathhouses.
Land status: State park
Fees and permits: Entrance fee under $5

Schedule: Open daily from 8:00 a.m. to sunset
Maps: Available at the ranger station
Trail contacts: John Pennekamp Coral Reef State Park, P.O. Box 487, Key Largo, FL 33037; (305) 451-1202 or www.floridastateparks.org/pennekamp

Mangrove Trail

Finding the trailhead: John Pennekamp Coral Reef State Park is located at Mile Marker 102.5 in Key Largo. Look for the big brown and white Pennekamp Park sign that looms over the roadway almost as soon as you arrive in Key Largo; you can't miss it. To find the Mangrove Trail, drive past the marina to the parking lot at Far Beach. **GPS:** N25 07.435' W080 24.169'

The Hike

Starting from the parking lot beside the Far Beach, you'll join a 0.37-mile boardwalk through a dense mangrove area. At the start, a bridge passes over a tidal creek. Tidal creeks normally are an overlooked part of the coastal landscape, but they perform a vital role in how a mangrove forest functions.

A mangrove tree forest contains an interlocking root system that provides a safe haven for numerous small fish and invertebrates, creating crucial coastal nurseries where many of South Florida's most popular gamefish can hide from predators as they grow. A tidal creek functions to bring in water and food at high tide, then flush the waterway system during the ebb tide.

After the tidal creek, you'll soon come to an observation tower beside the creek that offers a fine view of the mangrove treetops. With the roots obscured by the thick leaf canopy, it's not apparent three different types of mangroves grow here. The red mangroves, closest to the water, are known for their maze of red, interlocking roots humans find almost impossible to penetrate. Growing behind red mangroves are black mangroves, best identified by their shallow cable roots that extend from the tree and produce pneumato-

▶ **Pennekamp Park is named after a former publisher of the *Miami Herald*.**

phores that protrude finger-like above the soil. Closest to dry land are the white mangroves, which have a shallow root system making them vulnerable to extreme wind or wave action.

Because mangroves dominated the shoreline of so much potentially valuable waterfront property, developers targeted them for removal until the state finally stopped such wholesale environmental destruction. Mangrove thickets are annoying to humans because they are a favorite home of mosquitoes, but the variety of animals that inhabit them and associated waters is amazing: 181 species of birds, an estimated 220 species of fish, 18 mammal species, 24 species of reptiles and amphibians, and an unknown number of invertebrates like pink shrimp and spiny lobster.

The precise number of insects hasn't been established, either, but on a still, hot summer evening it seems each mangrove tree houses enough hungry mosquitoes to equal the population of China.

Miles and Directions

0.00 Start from last parking lot near Far Beach. Boardwalk starts in extreme right-hand corner.

0.04 Trail Ys. Go left.

0.10 Arrive at observation tower on the right.

0.32 Trail Ts. Go left to return to parking lot.

0.37 Arrive back at parking lot.

Wild Tamarind Trail

Finding the trailhead: The Wild Tamarind Trail leaves from the back (northeast corner) of the first parking lot on the right driving into Pennekamp Park; if you pass the marina and go over a bridge, you've missed the parking area, which is north and east of the marina. **GPS:** N25 07.530' W080 24.427'

The Hike

Entering the parking lot, park in the upper left-hand corner and look for the trailhead sign pointing to the natural pathway that goes through a surprisingly dense woodland. This well-marked nature walk is named for the extensive number of large tamarind trees along the hike. The trees produce a small white, fragrant flower that insects favor, which in turn attract many small birds during the spring (April) migration. After a rain, these trees are also a favorite for the Liguus tree snails that like to graze on the algae, fungi, and lichen growing on their bark. On my last series of Keys hikes, I found more tree snails here than anywhere else.

Poisonwood grows here, as well as some excellent species of gumbo limbo trees. Easily identified by their red peeling bark—which earned them the name "tourist trees" after visitors who stay in the sun too long—this wood is surprisingly lightweight and easy to carve. These characteristics, and their considerable girth, made them a favorite for making carousel horses in the 1800s and 1900s.

If you pass trees that appear to have scratch marks, you're probably seeing a pigeon plum tree, related to the better known seagrape tree. The scrapes are likely made by raccoons seeking the pigeon plum's purple fruits. Only the female trees produce them.

Early explorers considered one tree here of particular importance. It came to be known as the Spanish stopper. Its leaves were used to make a tea that cured diarrhea. It's also called the Spanish cork tree.

Miles and Directions

0.00 Standing in the northeast corner of the parking lot and facing the trees, look for a sign pointing to the trailhead.

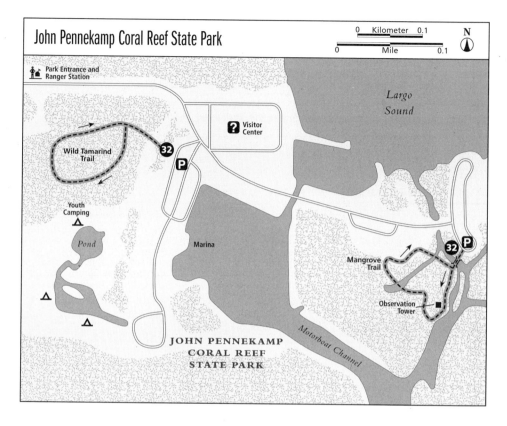

John Pennekamp Coral Reef State Park

0   Kilometer   0.1
0   Mile   0.1

N

Park Entrance and Ranger Station

Largo Sound

Visitor Center

Wild Tamarind Trail

32

P

Youth Camping

Pond

Marina

Mangrove Trail

32

P

Observation Tower

JOHN PENNEKAMP
CORAL REEF
STATE PARK

Motorboat Channel

0.11 Arrive at four-way cross. Go straight to reach bench and interpretive signs. Turn left to start trail walk.

0.23 Pass bench. Trail makes sharp right.

0.29 Trail makes a T. Go left to return to parking lot.

0.38 Arrive back at parking lot.

More Information

Local Information

Monroe County Tourist Development Council: www.fla-keys.com/keylargo.
Key Largo Chamber of Commerce: www.keylargochamber.org.

Local Events/Attractions

Four different **boat tours** can be arranged at the park marina. Weather permitting, 2.5-hour glass-bottom boat tours visit the offshore reef three times daily. Four-hour sailing and snorkeling tours aboard a 38-foot catamaran depart in the morning and afternoon. Half-day scuba tours visit two different dive spots. The park's dive shop is a PADI Resort Facility offering instruction and rental equipment.

Lodging

Lodging is available in Key Largo.

Camping

There are 47 full-facility sites for both tents and RVs. Maximum occupancy is 8 people per site. Pets are allowed in the campground. Reservations can be made up to 11 months in advance: (800) 326-3521 or www.reserveamerica.com.

Organizations

Florida Department of Environmental Protection/Division of Recreation and Parks: www.dep .state.fl.us/parks.

Florida Keys National Marine Sanctuary: http://floridakeys.noaa.gov.

Coral Reef Park Company: www.pennekamppark.com.

In the Florida Keys, thick mangrove swamps resemble the Everglades' sea of grass, inaccessible without the use of long boardwalks.

33 Windley Key Fossil Reef Geological State Park: Sunset and Hammock Trails

This park offers a chance to walk through more than 125,000 years of Keys history, going back to the time when the Key Largo limestone was formed as part of a massive coral reef when the sea was estimated to be 20 to 30 feet higher than today. Later, the sea level fell by an estimated 300 feet, and only between 5,000 and 6,000 years ago did the separate islets of the Keys appear as we know them today.

Windley Key was once two islands known as the Umbrella Keys. They became one when they were sold to Henry Flagler's Florida East Coast Railway for $852.80. Crews filled the shallow space between the two islands with chunks of fossilized reef removed from a quarry on Windley Key that provided many thousands of tons of fill for the rail bed and bridge approaches. The land continued to be used as a quarry until the 1960s. On your walk, you'll see decades of amazingly clean cuts by quarry machinery that have exposed flawlessly preserved fossils of the old reef and its inhabitants.

Three short trails wander through the quarries and a thirty-acre West Indian hardwood hammock with more than forty different kinds of trees. When the trees carry ripe fruit, they are a magnet for migratory birds. In winter, the park is a perfect place for a family outing.

Nearest town: Islamorada
Start: Visitor center
Distance: 1.4-mile lollipop loops
Approximate hiking time: 1 hour
Difficulty: Easy
Trail surface: Natural (in this case, rocky)
Seasons: December to April
Other trail users: Trail walkers only
Canine compatibility: No pets

Land status: State park
Fees and permits: Entrance fee under $5
Schedule: Open Thursday to Monday only, from 8:00 a.m. to 5:00 p.m.
Maps: Available at the entrance
Trail contacts: Windley Key Fossil Reef Geological State Park, P.O. Box 1052, Islamorada, FL 33036; (305) 664-2540 or www.floridastateparks.org/windleykey

Finding the trailhead: The park is located at Mile Marker 85.5 on Windley Key near Islamorada. **GPS:** N24 57.004' W080 35.733'

The Hike

Two musts on this pleasant walk: Pick up (and return) the interpretive brochure, and bring a camera because you probably won't believe the number of fossilized coral skeletons you'll see on the quarry walls—and beneath your feet on the pathway. They are particularly evident in the first segment through the Windley Quarry. After supplying bedrock for Flagler's railroad, the Windley Quarry was mined for decorative stones imbedded with fossilized brain coral, star coral, and small cup coral.

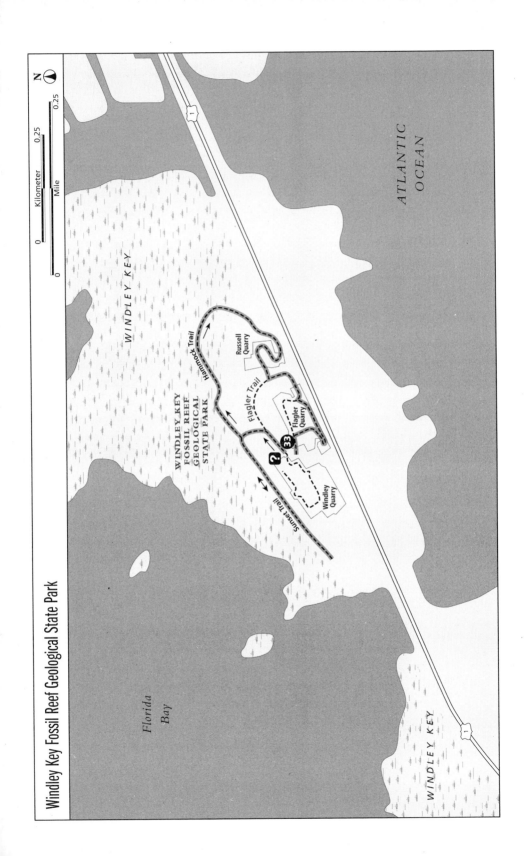

Windley Key Fossil Reef Geological State Park

The Sunset and Hammock Trails both leave from the visitor center. Take time to examine the rusted remains of the channeling machine used to cut coral by raising and lowering two sets of parallel-hardened chisels about 6 inches deep as it moved down the tracks. Reaching the end, the machine was moved back to the beginning and the chisels set about 6 inches deeper for each pass until they had sunk from 8 to 10 feet deep. Salt water was pumped into the channels to clean them of any debris. It all seems very primitive, but the system worked.

At the start, the two trails overlap for a good distance before separating. Go left on the Sunset Trail skirting the top of the Windley Quarry, then follow the path down through a mangrove thicket. You'll also encounter Keys thatch palms, though not in the same number as in Curry Hammock State Park.

Once the Sunset Trail ends, retrace your steps to the junction with the Hammock Trail and where you turned left. Join the Hammock Trail, where the limestone base contains a sizable number of solution holes, bowl-shaped depressions caused by erosion. Here, as every-where in the park, the trees are fairly stunted, unable to reach their normal height because they grow on a limestone base. One of the taller trees is the gumbo limbo tree, also called the "tourist tree" because its peeling red bark resembles the skin of a first-time visitor to Florida.

▶ While it's not legal to remove fossils, you can make rubbings of the quarry walls

Because solution holes in the limestone bedrock can hold water, early settlers used them for planting different trees, which explains why you find yourself surrounded by many types of plum trees such as jungle, hog, and pigeon plums. Most are too sour for human tastes but raccoons and birds definitely like them; so, look for animals in this section.

As you leave the Hammock Trail and move into the Russell Quarry, you'll find the remnants of an old homesteader's well on the right. Instead of directly returning to the visitor center on the Hammock Trail, go left for a quick tour of the Flagler Quarry with even more fossilized corals and a number of shaded picnic tables. Bear to the left and go along the quarry wall to find the old quarry station foundation and cradles for water tanks. End the walk by taking a ramp back to the parking lot.

Miles and Directions

0.0 Start from the visitor center where Sunset and Hammock Trails overlap.

0.3 Sunset and Hammock Trails separate. Go left onto Sunset Trail.

0.5 Sunset Trail ends. Retrace steps.

0.7 Reach junction with Hammock Trail. Go straight.

1.0 Pass bench; go straight.

1.2 Pass shaded bench; go straight.

1.4 Trail ends at parking lot.

More Information

Local Information

Islamorada Chamber of Commerce: www.islamoradachamber.com.

Monroe County Tourist Development Council: www.fla-keys.com/islamorada.

Local Events/Attractions

Guided tours of the quarry are conducted Thursday through Monday at 10:00 a.m. and 2:00 p.m. The park's Alison Fahrer Environmental Education Center has **displays** on Flagler's railroad, Florida Keys' geology, and tropical hardwood hammocks.

A quarry on the ocean side of the key has been turned into a performing area for the **Theater of the Sea** (Mile Marker 84.5), one of the Keys' oldest attractions. Like SeaWorld in Orlando, it offers various animal shows and the chance to swim with bottlenose dolphins.

Lodging

Islamorada Chamber of Commerce: www.islamoradachamber.com.

Monroe County Tourist Development Council: www.fla-keys.com/islamorada.

Camping

Depending on which way you're driving, campsites are available at Long Key State Park or John Pennekamp Coral Reef State Park.

Organizations

Florida Department of Environmental Protection/Division of Recreation and Parks: www.dep.state.fl.us/parks.

Friends of Islamorada Area State Parks, Inc.: P.O. Box 236, Islamorada, FL 33036.

34 Lignumvitae Key Botanical State Park: Nature Trail

Offshore, at Lignumvitae Key, is one of the best places in the Keys to find the elusive Liguus snails, whose shells were once worth a small fortune.

At 16.5 feet above sea level, Lignumvitae Key enjoys one of the highest elevations in the Keys. The 280-acre offshore key in the Gulf of Mexico boasts a virgin tropical forest not found anywhere else in the Keys. The tropical hammock contains typical West Indian trees, including the endangered lignumvitae, which is said to live a thousand years. Lignumvitae wood is incredibly durable, assumed to outlast steel or bronze thanks to its rich resins.

Some very fanciful myths surround the lignumvitae tree. In the fifteenth century it was cataloged as a tree found in the Garden of Eden and thought to be the wood used to make the Holy Grail (though other sources say the grail was made of metal). In the Bahamas lignumvitae is still known as "holywood" and is said to cure impotence. Mature trees usually bloom the first two weeks of April with half-inch blue flowers.

Nearest town: Islamorada
Start: By boat from Mile Marker 77.5
Distance: 1.3-mile loop
Approximate hiking time: Full tour, 1.5 hours
Difficulty: Easy
Trail surface: Hard surface leading to trail-head; natural surface for the hike
Seasons: Winter is best for walking.
Other trail users: Hikers only
Canine compatibility: No pets except service animals
Land status: State park

Fees and permits: Entrance fee under $5
Schedule: Open Thursday through Monday
8:00 a.m. to 5:00 p.m.
Access: By charter boat or rental kayak or
canoe available from Robbie's Marina at Mile
Marker 77.5. For tour reservations call (305)
664-9814. Boats run from 9:00 a.m. and stop
at 3:30 p.m.
Maps: Not available

Trail contacts: Lignumvitae Key Botanical State Park, P.O. Box 1052, Islamorada,
FL 33036; (305) 664-2540 or www.florida
stateparks.org/lignumvitaekey. Access to the
trail is restricted to ranger-guided walks offered
at 10:00 a.m. and 2:00 p.m. Tour boats depart
Robbie's Marina thirty minutes before the
walks.

Finding the trailhead: The park is located at Mile Marker 78.5, a mile offshore and northwest of Upper Matecumbe Key. Tour boats operate at 9:30 a.m. and 1:30 p.m. Thursday through
Monday. Check ahead for the specific schedule and fee. If the tour boat is not running, rentals are
available at Robbie's Marina at Mile Marker 77.5. A scheduled tour lasts 1.5 hours. **GPS:** N24
54.180' W080 41.736'

The Hike

The tour boat docks at the Matheson House, belonging to the family that owned
the island between 1919 and 1953. Their limestone house was built of fireproof coral
rock, which made it possible to include the kitchen inside the house. A windmill
and 12,000-gallon cistern still stand, surrounded by such West Indian trees as mastic,
sapodilla, and banyan.

The thick forest hammock contains more than sixty-five different tree species:
gumbo limbo, poisonwood, and strangler fig, all true natives of the Caribbean. It's
believed they arrived here as seeds from other tropical islands, carried by waves, by
wind, or in the digestive tracts of migratory birds. The
seeds sprouted and began the endless cycle of birth,
death, and decay that transformed this once-barren
coral island to a miniature jungle.

▶ **Insects are at their peak
May through November.**

Many islands of the Upper Keys once contained
similar growth, but unfortunately it was deliberately
destroyed for one of the most bizarre reasons imaginable: to increase the value of the
snails collected from the different hammocks.

Hardwood hammocks throughout the Keys once housed Liguus tree snails, whose
colorful shells were highly prized by collectors around the world. Because the snails
from different hammocks had different color patterns on their shells, collectors would
take a sampling from a particular location, then set fire to the hammock to increase
the rarity/price of that snail variety. The tree snails found on Lignumvitae carry bands
of red and green on their cream-colored shells.

You'll see two remarkable sights on this walk. One is a low stone fence that
extends for almost 1.5 miles. Its purpose, and who built it, may not be known, but
you have to admire the amount of labor that went into constructing it. Even more
noteworthy is the nation's largest lignumvitae tree, an estimated 1,000 years old.

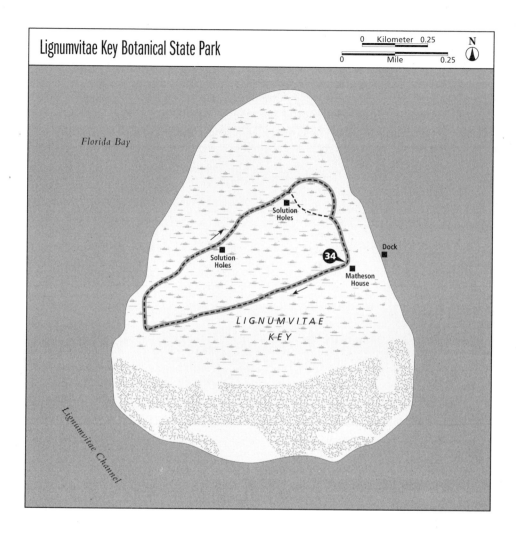

Lignumvitae Key Botanical State Park

0 Kilometer 0.25
0 Mile 0.25

N

Florida Bay

Solution Holes

Solution Holes

Dock

34

Matheson House

LIGNUMVITAE KEY

Lignumvitae Channel

Miles and Directions

0.0 Start from the Matheson House.

0.6 Pass wall made of limestone.

1.0 Trail junction. Go left to continue return loop.

1.3 End at Matheson House.

More Information

Local Information

Islamorada Chamber of Commerce: www.islamoradachamber.com.

Monroe County Tourist Development Council: www.fla-keys.com/islamorada.

Local Events/Attractions

If you want to do more **island-hopping** by boat, it's also possible to visit Indian Key Historic Site, which sits a short distance from Upper Matecumbe on the Atlantic side. Indian Key is a considerably smaller island that began as a wrecking station, then became the Dade County Seat in 1836. Ruins of an old town are still evident. The vegetation here is markedly different from Lignumvitae Key, since agaves and other desert-dwelling plants were introduced on Indian Key in the 1800s and allowed to replace many of the native plants. You'll find a self-guided tour path to lead you around the island; formal tours are not provided. You'll need to rent your own boat to reach Indian Key.

Lodging

Lodging is available in nearby Islamorada.

Camping

The closest camping sites are located at Long Key State Park. Sixty full facility campsites are lined up along the water, many well shaded by tall Australian Pines. Make reservations up to eleven months in advance: (800) 326-3521 or www.reserveamerica.com.

Organizations

Florida Department of Environmental Protection/Division of Recreation and Parks: www.dep .state.fl.us/parks.

Friends of Islamorada Area State Parks, Inc.: P.O. Box 236, Islamorada, FL 33036.

35 Long Key State Park: Golden Orb and Layton Trails

Long Key, a narrow ribbon of park containing 965 acres, could just as easily have been named Narrow Key. In some places the oceanfront boundary is only a hundred yards from U.S. Highway 1, and the traffic is clearly visible from the beach. The Spanish called Long Key *Cayo Vivora,* meaning "Rattlesnake Key." Fortunately, this description applied more to the shape of the island—a rattlesnake with its jaws open—than the resident fauna. Wading birds and raccoons are the most commonly seen animals.

▶ **Henry Flagler established the Long Key Fishing Club, which drew top anglers from everywhere. Among them was a dentist-turned-western-novelist, Zane Gray, who had a particular fondness for stalking bonefish, the gray ghost of the flats. The club was destroyed by the great hurricane of 1935.**

These two short nature trails go through some of the most beautiful natural scenery in the Keys. The trees growing along the trails are of Caribbean origin, including the peeling red bark of the famous gumbo limbo tree and poisonwood, mahogany, Jamaica dogwood, and crabwood. The Calusa Indians used them all for special purposes, some of them now outlawed. The Jamaica dogwood, for instance, was also called the fish poison tree since its gray bark and green leaves could be used to stun and asphyxiate fish. So much for "sport" fishing.

The seeds of the crabwood produce an oil with several homeopathic uses: as a remedy for dandruff and rashes and as a laxative. It's also used as an insect repellent and moisturizer, making it a very versatile tree. Unless you know how to quickly extract crabwood oil, be sure to carry a bottle of insect repellent. At the beginning and end of the Golden Orb Trail, the walk goes through dense mangroves, which often house many mosquitoes.

Nearest town: Layton
Start: Respective parking lots
Distance: 1.03-mile loop, 0.20-mile loop
Approximate hiking time: 40 minutes, 15 minutes
Difficulty: Easy
Trail surface: Hard surface leading to trailhead; natural surface for the hike
Seasons: Winter is best for walking.
Other trail users: Hikers only
Canine compatibility: Pets not allowed on

beaches, in picnic shelters, or bathhouses. Leashed pets are permitted on nature trail and in camping area.
Land status: State park
Fees and permits: Entrance fee under $5
Schedule: Open daily from 8:00 a.m. to sunset
Maps: Available at the ranger station
Trail contacts: Long Key State Park, P.O. Box 776, Long Key, FL 33001; (305) 664-4815 or www.floridastateparks.org/longkey

The Golden Orb Trail at Long Key State Park starts on a boardwalk in a mangrove swamp and ends in a dry sandy area inhabited by numerous hermit crabs.

Golden Orb Trail

Finding the trailhead: Follow US 1 south to Mile Marker 67.5. The park entrance is on the left. Once inside the park, take the turnoff on the left to reach the Golden Orb Trail/Boardwalk. If you arrive at the water without making a turn, you've gone too far. **GPS:** N24 48.851' W080 49.285'

The Hike

The Golden Orb Trail, taking about forty minutes to complete, is accessed by a boardwalk that penetrates a dense mangrove forest. An observation platform about midway along the boardwalk offers an excellent overview of the region, though you'll probably see mostly mangrove tops and a few birds in flight.

At the end of the boardwalk is a section where you can camp as the Seminoles did: On both sides of the boardwalk, quite close to one another, are a handful of thatch-covered platforms with open sides. These are chickees, the type of home once used by Florida's Seminole Indians.

The only way to sleep comfortably on these wooden platforms is with a thick air mattress. If the wind dies, expect mosquitoes to swarm out of the mangroves and attempt to transfuse all your blood—into themselves. A far better choice for camping here would be the regular sandy campsites shaded by a canopy of Australian pines that are guaranteed to lull you to sleep as they rustle in the breeze.

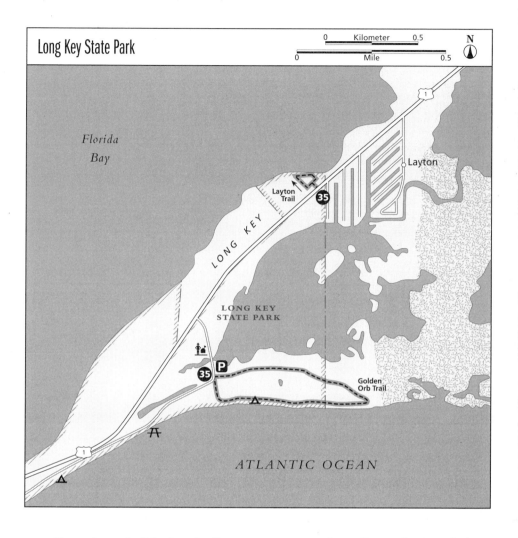

Kilometer 0.5

Mile 0.5

N

Florida Bay

Layton

Layton Trail

35

LONG KEY

LONG KEY STATE PARK

P 35

Golden Orb Trail

1

ATLANTIC OCEAN

From the end of the boardwalk, retrace your steps just a few yards to reach the Golden Orb trailhead. Step down off the boardwalk to start the path located on the right (north). The trail is named for the large golden orb weaver spider commonly seen on this walk. The golden orb spider weaves the most conspicuous webs of any Florida spider. The females, usually about one hundred times larger than the males, do all the weaving. It obviously requires a large amount of energy since the spider often eats its old web before building a new one. The females will also eat the tiny males when food becomes scarce.

Don't be put off by its dining habits: The spider is extremely colorful and easy to photograph thanks to its considerable size (some may be the size of your palm). Also called the golden silk and banana spider, the golden orb spider is the largest non-tarantula spider in North America.

The Golden Orb path leads through different types of Keys' plant communities. After crossing a mangrove creek, it follows a sandy berm above the narrow beach. From this vantage, it's easy to see the transition from salt-tolerant plants on the low ground to the tropical hammock on the higher ground. The return loop passes through a large mangrove area before venturing into a hardwood forest near the end of the walk. Hermit crabs are common in the sandy sections but should not be removed.

Miles and Directions

0.00 Start from front of parking lot near boardwalk and restrooms.

0.08 Reach observation platform.

0.14 Reach Golden Orb trailhead. Go left.

0.19 Cross tidal creek on boardwalk.

0.26 Trail moves away from beach.

0.33 Walk sandy berm beside beach.

0.48 Pass shaded bench.

0.71 Pass bench in open sun.

0.88 Enter tropical hardwood hammock.

1.03 Emerge at rear of parking lot.

Layton Trail

Finding the trailhead: The Layton Trail starts off US 1 at Mile Marker 67.7, on the Gulf side. This is about a half-mile north of the park's main entrance. **GPS:** N24 49.381' W080 49.059'

The Hike

Where the Golden Orb Trail skirts the Atlantic side, the Layton Trail goes in the opposite direction, to the west, where it meets the huge expanse known as Florida Bay extending from the Keys to the Everglades. More birds are typically seen on the Gulf side, particularly flocks of pelicans. The Layton Trail is only about a fifteen-minute walk, round-trip. Be careful when the path follows the limestone shoreline. The rock is often covered with slippery seaweed.

Miles and Directions

0.00 Start from car parked on side of road.

0.05 Reach Florida Bay.

0.20 Return to trailhead.

More Information

Local Information

Islamorada Chamber of Commerce: www.islamoradachamber.com.
Monroe County Tourist Development Council: www.fla-keys.com/marathon.

Local Events/Attractions

The Long Key Lakes Canoe Trail marks a leisurely "paddle" through a shallow water lagoon. **Canoe rentals** and a self-guided brochure are available. The trip takes about an hour.

Two special ranger programs are offered October to July: a two-hour **guided walk** on the Golden Orb Trail Wednesday at 10:00 a.m. and a Ranger's Choice program Thursday at 10:00 a.m., which may involve guided walks, birding, photography, Florida's Native Americans, canoeing, or Florida's unique wildlife. Program selection is based on ranger availability and weather conditions. Call (305) 664-4815 for details about either.

Lodging

Accommodations are available in Islamorada or Marathon.

Camping

Long Key State Park is my favorite place to camp in all the Keys. Sixty full facility campsites are lined up along the water, many well shaded by tall Australian Pines. Reservations can be made up to eleven months in advance: (800) 326-3521 or www.reserveamerica.com.

Organizations

Florida Department of Environmental Protection/Division of Recreation and Parks: www.dep .state.fl.us/parks.

Friends of Islamorada Area State Parks, Inc. (citizen support organization): P.O. Box 236, Islamorada, FL 33036.

36 Curry Hammock State Park: Nature Trail

Overall, thatch palm is scarce these days because so much of it was used to make roofs for homes and bars. At Curry Hammock, thatch palm trees are still abundant.

One of Florida's newer state parks, Curry Hammock encompasses more than a thousand acres on five different islands in the Middle Keys. It contains one of the largest remaining stands of Florida thatch palm in North America. This small- to medium-size tree, native to the lower Florida Keys and many Caribbean islands, has shiny light green leaves that were overharvested to make waterproof thatch roofs.

The Curry Hammock Nature Trail is probably the hardest of the Keys' hikes, literally, due to all the broken and uneven limestone terrain forming the trail path. Although the trail lacks any incline, you will encounter plenty of declines in the numerous limestone potholes that pockmark the land. This Swiss-cheese landscape contains endless opportunities to trip and fall on your face if you don't watch the trail. This definitely is not a path for flip-flops or open-toe sandals. Tennis shoes are needed.

Nearest town: Marathon
Start: Gravel parking lot at Mile Marker 55.2
Distance: 1.25-mile lollipop loop
Approximate hiking time: 1 hour
Difficulty: Easy, but be careful on the uneven limestone.
Trail surface: Hard surface leading to trailhead; natural surface for the hike
Seasons: Winter
Other trail users: Hikers only
Canine compatibility: Pets are not allowed

on beaches, in the water, or in picnic shelters. Leashed pets are permitted on nature trail.
Land status: State park
Fees and permits: Entrance fee under $5
Schedule: Open daily from 8:00 a.m. to sunset
Maps: Available at the ranger station
Trail contacts: Curry Hammock State Park, 56200 Overseas Highway, Marathon, FL 33050; (305)289-2690 or www.florida stateparks.org/curryhammock

Finding the trailhead: The park is located along both sides of U.S. Highway 1 starting at Little Crawl Key, Mile Marker 56.2, 11 miles west of Long Key. The entrance to the facilities is on the ocean side of US 1. The nature trail is not reached through the park's main entrance. Instead, the access path is located a mile south of the park. Park at the small gravel parking area off US 1 on the Gulf side. **GPS:** N24 44.527' W80 59.747'

The Hike

This is a good example of a rockland hammock where solid limestone rock is just under the surface. The shallow soil limits the size of trees that grow here, but it obviously is well suited for the thousands of thatch palms that grow here. The uneven surface makes it necessary to watch where you're stepping since parts of the trail are heavily pocked with holes. Look for hermit crabs and some colorful (usually harmless) snakes.

The walk begins on a short segment of the hard surfaced Florida Keys Overseas Heritage Trail that starts in Key West and runs the length of the Keys (see sidebar). Once you start on the Curry Hammock Nature Trail, you move into a well-shaded, interior part of Fat Deer Key. The trail is easy to follow, outlined in small limestone rocks that make this resemble a neatly landscaped palm garden.

▶ **The trail is located on Fat Deer Key, which is considered part of the city of Marathon.**

Just before the midpoint, you'll see a short side trail that leads to Florida Bay, which is much closer than it seems. Take advantage of the short detour to see if there is a good breeze blowing that will cool you off; the dense interior can be very still. If you're lucky, you'll see a Key Vaca raccoon, a threatened species found only in the Middle Keys. Smaller than a normal raccoon, it favors the mangrove shoreline.

On the return loop, the trail is even more winding and twisting. One of the major features here is a large section of solution holes. They help bring into perspective the impact of global warming and how everything is cyclical. About 120,000 years ago, the ocean was about 20 feet deep here and the limestone you walk on was part of a massive coral reef.

But then the glaciers froze and the water dropped an estimated 300 feet, which allowed the Keys to become part of the mainland. Conditions changed again, and within the last 6,000 years, the Keys became the string of islands they are today.

FLORIDA KEYS OVERSEAS HERITAGE TRAIL: WORK IN PROGRESS

The small size of most Keys islands determines that most walks are short ones of a mile or two with one important exception: The Florida Keys Overseas Heritage Trail. Intended for bicycle and pedestrian use, the trail is still under design and construction. When complete, it will run for 106 miles from Key West to Key Largo.

Paralleling US 1, the trail will make use of the old bridge system to create a safe corridor that largely avoids mainstream traffic. Ultimately, the trail system is envisioned as incorporating a wide variety of activities including hiking, running, bicycling, in-line skating, sightseeing, and fishing. Water access points will also allow kayaking.

Less than half the length is open. Latest information is available online at the Office of Greenways and Trails, www.dep.state.fl.us/gwt/state/keystrail. Also at Florida Keys Overseas Heritage Trail, 3 La Croix Court, Key Largo, FL 33037; (305) 853-3571. Tallahassee headquarters: (850) 245-2052.

The Overseas Heritage Trail is a bicycle and pedestrian trail, which, when completed, will run for 106 miles from Key West to Key Largo.

Miles and Directions

0.00 Start at parking lot. Go right to join the Overseas Heritage Trail.

0.15 Turn left at info kiosk.

0.21 Turn left to join trailhead.

0.36 T junction. Go left.

0.40 Trail makes a Y. Go right.

0.55 Trail curves to start return loop.

0.60 Go left on side trail to Florida Bay.

0.62 Reach Florida Bay. Retrace steps.

0.64 Reach main loop. Go left.

0.86 Trail comes in from left. Go left to parking lot.

1.04 Return to trailhead. Go right to kiosk.

1.10 Reach kiosk; go right.

1.25 Arrive back at parking lot.

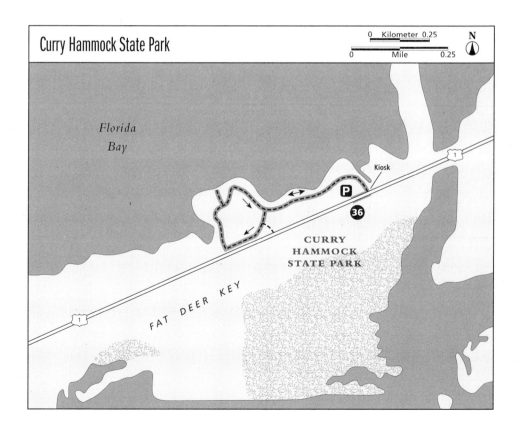

More Information

Local Information

Monroe County Tourist Development Council: www.fla-keys.com/marathon.

Local Events/Attractions

Bicycles are allowed on park roads and the Overseas Heritage Trail that passes through the park. Persons under sixteen years must wear a bike helmet. Bicycles are limited to roadways and are not permitted on footpaths, boardwalks, restroom ramps, or the nature trail.

Canoes and kayaks can be launched from both the day-use area and campground; there are miles of shoreline on both the Atlantic and Florida Bay sides. No facilities for powerboats are available in the park. Most waters in the park are a no-combustion zone.

Inline skating is possible on both the park's roadways and on the Overseas Heritage Trail.

This is a prime **birding** area. Raptors are often seen during migration periods. Hawk Watch International sponsors a census of the raptors passing through the park each fall. The endangered white-crowned pigeon frequents the area in summer to feed on poisonwood berries.

Lodging

Lodging is available in Marathon, in the Middle Keys.

Camping

The 28-site campground, located along the oceanfront in the main park, is open only part of the year, from November 1 through May 31. Sites have a gravel parking area and adjoining sand area for a tent. Reservations can be made through Reserve America at (866) I CAMP FL (866-422-6735) or www.reserveamerica.com up to eleven months in advance.

Organizations

Florida Department of Environmental Protection/Division of Recreation and Parks: www.dep .state.fl.us/parks.

Friends of Islamorada Area State Parks Inc. (citizen support organization): P. O. Box 236, Islamorada, FL 33036.

37 Marathon Bridge Walk: Old Seven Mile Bridge to Pigeon Key

Pigeon Key is a small island of about five and one-third acres situated under a section of the old Seven Mile Bridge and adjacent to the new. The old Seven Mile Bridge, built for Henry Flagler's Overseas Railroad, was considered the Eighth Wonder of the World. Pigeon Key, sometimes called Pigeon Island, played an important role in the railroad's construction, the temporary home to many of the railway workers.

Owned by Monroe County, the island is properly known as the Pigeon Key National Historic District. A nonprofit group is in the process of restoring seven of the historical buildings used by the railroaders. The island's largest building, the Old Section Gang Quarters, was restored at a cost of $300,000. A small museum highlighting the railroad era also is open.

▶ Pigeon Island was probably named after the white-crowned pigeon.

It's possible to take a small train (The Pigeon Key Express) to the island from Mile Marker 47 on Knight Key. But a better way is to walk to Pigeon Key taking the Old Seven Mile Bridge.

Nearest town: Marathon
Start: Parking lot at the end of the old bridge
Distance: 4.4 miles out and back
Approximate hiking time: 2 hours
Difficulty: Easy to moderate, depending on humidity and heat and whether you have water, sunblock, and a hat.
Trail surface: Hard pavement
Seasons: Winter is best for walking.
Other trail users: Anglers, "Henry" the tour tram

Canine compatibility: No pets
Land status: Owned by Monroe County; on the National Register of Historic Places
Fees and permits: Entrance fee under $10
Schedule: Museum open 10:00 a.m. to 5:00 p.m.
Maps: None needed
Trail contact: Pigeon Key Foundation, P.O. Box 500130, Marathon, FL 33050; (305) 289-0025; www.pigeonkey.net

Finding the trailhead: Going south, the old section of the Seven Mile Bridge is the one on the right (north)—the one without all the traffic. The bridge is a favorite fishing spot. Parking is available near the bridge entrance. **GPS:** N24 42.436' W081 7.491'

The Hike

This is a rare opportunity to peer down into clear Keys waters from a high vantage point and not have to worry about traffic. The surface of the old road heats up during the day, so wear good shoes and a hat, and bring water. On your walk to Pigeon Key, you'll see quite a few boats tied up to the old bridge pilings. After twenty to thirty minutes, you'll be able to look down on the island itself.

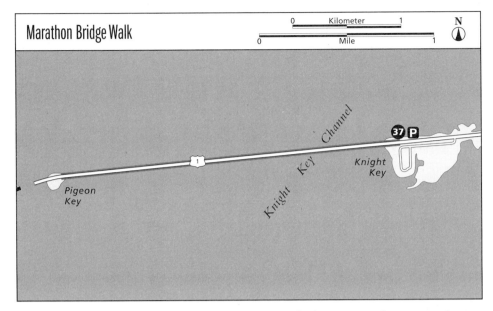

A short paved road on the left leads down to the key. No need to worry about missing the turn-off since the span of old bridge just beyond the key abruptly ends where a section was sliced away to make through motor traffic impossible.

Only a few feet above sea level, tiny, very flat Pigeon Key makes you aware of the problems of hurricane storm surge and why many residents pack up and leave as soon as they realize the Keys are in the path of a storm. Fortunately, most of the old buildings here have survived everything Mother Nature has thrown their way, though they definitely have been weathered. This is one of the few surviving historic sites in the Keys from the early 1900s.

Flagler bought Pigeon Island in 1909, and by 1912 it was a crowded, bustling place with four bunkhouses holding sixty-four men each and numerous tents set up over wooden floors on stilts. There was also an engineering office. After the railroad was completed, the island served as bridge tender maintenance camp. Homes, a school, and a post office were added. Following the devastating hurricane of 1935, Pigeon Key was an important hub for the construction of U.S. Highway 1 over Flagler's rail bed.

The Pigeon Key Foundation was established to preserve the island and has restored many of its buildings. The historical museum operates from the assistant bridge tender's house. Overall, plan on spending about an hour to explore the island. This is in addition to the round-trip bridge walk.

Miles and Directions

0.0 Start from parking lot at end of old bridge.

2.2 Arrive at Pigeon Key.

4.4 Walk ends back at parking lot.

More Information

Local Information

Monroe County Tourist Development Council: www.fla-keys.com/marathon.

Local Events/Attractions

The **visitor center** is open 10:00 a.m. to 5:00 p.m. daily at Mile Marker 47 on Knight Key. **Tours** of the island depart hourly from 10:00 a.m. to 4:00 p.m.

The Florida Keys Ocean Science Center based at Pigeon Key offers **science and research programs** for students and teachers. Overnight packages range from three-day/two-night to five-day/four-night programs.

Some visitors bring their masks and **snorkels** and a picnic lunch to spend half a day on the island.

Lodging

Lodging is available in Marathon.

Camping

Campsites are available in Long Key State Park.

Organizations

Florida Keys Ocean Science Center at Pigeon Key: www.pigeonkey.net.

38 Bahia Honda State Park: Silver Palm and Old Bridge Trails

Bahia Honda State Park offers both a nature walk paralleling its award-winning beach and a section of Old U.S. Highway 1.

In the Keys sandy beaches are as rare as winning lottery tickets, but 524–acre Bahia Honda State Park enjoys what is considered to be one of the finest beaches in the nation. Bahia Honda, Florida's southernmost state park, contains a natural environment found nowhere else in the continental United States.

> ▶ **Bahia Honda is the southernmost key where the ancient reef forming the Keys is exposed.**

Mangrove forest, beach dune, tropical hardwood hammock, and coastal berm communities all are found here. Many of the resident animals and plants have a Caribbean origin, which makes this a truly unusual ecosystem. Furthermore, the bird life is varied: roseate spoonbills, great white herons, white-crowned pigeons, reddish egrets, and least terns are frequently sighted.

This park is usually crowded on weekends, with people often turned away after 10:00 a.m.

Nearest town: Big Pine Key
Start: Each starts from its parking lot.
Distance: 0.50 mile loop, 0.47 mile out and back
Approximate hiking time: 1 hour for both
Difficulty: Easy
Trail surface: Mostly natural surface
Seasons: Winter
Other trail users: Hikers only
Canine compatibility: Pets are not allowed on beaches or in the water, picnic shelters, bathhouses, or cabins. Leashed pets are permitted on the nature trail and in the camping area.
Land status: State park
Fees and permits: Entrance fee under $5
Schedule: Open daily from 8:00 a.m. to sunset
Maps: Available at the ranger station
Trail contact: Bahia Honda State Park, 36850 Overseas Highway, Big Pine Key, FL 33043; (305) 872-2353; www.floridastateparks.org/bahiahonda

Silver Palm Nature Trail

Finding the trailhead: Bahia Honda is located 12 miles south of Marathon on US 1. After entering the park, turn left and follow the road to the end. The Silver Palm Nature Trail begins just beyond the parking lot. **GPS:** N24 39.889' W081 15.455'

The Hike

This 0.5-mile, twenty-minute loop walk leads into a mangrove area, over a dune, and down onto the beach. It's mostly open, so wear a hat and sunglasses. In more than a dozen places, the trail is marked with numbered posts explaining the landscape; be sure to obtain the trail guide available at the entrance station. The silver palms for which the trail is named are easy to spot since the fronds glare with a silver sheen in the direct rays of the sun. Silver palms are increasingly rare as they are removed from the wild for landscaping. Bahia Honda has one of the largest concentrations in Florida.

But for how much longer? This landscape is being taken over by a tropical hardwood hammock that could eventually shade out the silver palms with a dense growth of gumbo limbo, poisonwood, Jamaica dogwood, and other hardwoods—unless the hardwoods are reduced by fire, a tropical storm, or pruning by the park service.

The tropical hardwood hammock growing here was created by the seeds carried from South America and the Caribbean by the Gulf Stream. These seeds can often be seen in the seaweed mats along the beach. As unsightly as the seaweed may be, when it decays it does serve as a fertilizer for beach plants and sea grasses, and it also helps trap sand along the beach.

Although the Atlantic beach certainly deserves its title, it's best enjoyed during the cooler months when the prevailing winds sweep the seaweed away from shore. In summer the prevailing winds often cause the seaweed to clump up on the beach, and since seaweed is a natural part of the environment, park officials leave it for the winds and tides to dispose of. Should you arrive when seaweed is a problem, keep in mind there is a second beach on the Gulf side that's normally seaweed free and almost as pretty. The water feels equally refreshing in both places.

Miles and Directions

0.00 Depart from parking lot.

0.10 Side trail to mangrove shallows.

0.12 Trail makes sharp right.

0.15 Pass access path to beach on right.

0.23 Excellent example of silver palm tree on left, well back from trail.

0.28 Arrive at Bahia Honda beach; go right.

0.48 Reach boardwalk leading off beach.

0.50 End at parking lot.

Bahia Honda Old Bridge Walk

Finding the trailhead: Start at the southwest end of the island near the middle of the Calusa parking lot. Follow the sign pointing to the outdoor amphitheater. **GPS:** N24 39.271' W081 16.914'

The Hike

This short walk will take you to a short span of the Overseas Highway that offers an excellent view of the park. Walking this span will illustrate why a new bridge was badly needed here for so many years. It was, after all, never intended to be a modern highway but was built on top of the tracks of Henry Flagler's famed "Railroad That Went to Sea."

The walk starts at the southwest end of the island in the Calusa area near the middle of the parking lot. You'll walk up a steep path that leads to the park's open amphitheatre, where rangers hold programs every Friday evening (for campers only). Turn right to walk through a narrow stretch of trees and plants that butterflies often frequent.

You'll soon arrive at the short span of the old US 1 bridge that crosses Bahia Honda channel. *Bahia Honda* is Spanish for "deep bay," and the early explorers knew full well what they were talking about. Building the bridges across 5,055 feet of the channel's fast-moving water reaching depths of 35 feet was one of Flagler's biggest challenges. Notice the arched steel truss spans holding up the span; they were gigantic for their day.

Bahia Honda State Park

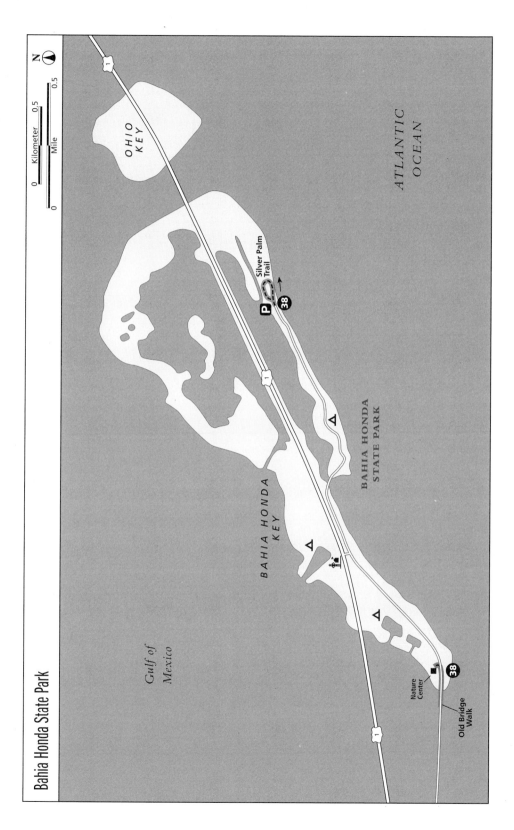

Consider what driving was like on old US 1 when this narrow thoroughfare was often clogged with RVs. Seems insane now, and it could be very scary. After a look around, it's time to retrace your steps and return to the parking lot.

Miles and Directions

0.00 Start from Calusa area parking lot.

0.03 Turn right at open air amphitheater.

0.13 Arrive at beginning of bridge.

0.23 Bridge ends; retrace steps.

0.44 Turn left at open air amphitheatre.

0.47 Arrive back at parking lot.

More Information

Local Information
Monroe County Tourist Development Council: www.fla-keys.com/lowerkeys.

Local Events/Attractions
The Sand and Sea Nature Center has a **sea life display**, small marine **aquarium**, and several **environmental activities**, as well as background information on the Keys. The Center is open 9:00 a.m. to 4:00 p.m. daily (closed for lunch from noon to 1:00 p.m.). The staff is extremely helpful.

Snorkeling in the 4- to 6-feet shallows just offshore may show soft corals, coral heads, tropical fish, queen conch, and spiny lobsters. Remember, queen conch are protected. Do not remove.

In-line skating is permitted on the park's 3.5-mile roadway. Sit-on-top rental **kayaks** are available at the park concession.

Lodging
Motels are available in Big Pine Key just south of Bahia Honda State Park. The park has 3 duplex cabins on stilts that each hold up to 6 people. Cabins are equipped with kitchen appliances, utensils, and linens. Most have central A/C and heat, two bedrooms, living room with sofa bed, kitchen/dining room, and full bath. The road leading to the cabins cannot handle vehicles over 6'8". Make reservations up to eleven months in advance at Reserve America at (800) 326-3521 or www.reserveamerica.com.

Camping
Three different campgrounds with up to 80 sites are located within the park. The specifics are so varied for each campground you need to check the park Web site at www.floridastateparks.org/bahiahonda/activities.cfm. Reservations can be made up to eleven months in advance at Reserve America at 800-326-3521 or www.reserveamerica.com.

Organizations
Florida Department of Environmental Protection/Division of Recreation and Parks: www.dep.state.fl.us/parks.

39 National Key Deer Refuge: Blue Hole and Nature Trails

At National Key Deer Refuge, come early or late to see the endangered Key deer, which number about 800 animals, up from a one-time low of fewer than 50.

The Keys is an amazing place, but probably one of the most peculiar locations is Big Pine Key in the Lower Keys, the hub of the National Key Deer Refuge. The refuge, established in 1957, encompasses 8,542 acres that also includes part of adjacent No Name Key. Despite the building boom on Big Pine Key, 2,278 acres are still designated as wilderness.

National Key Deer Refuge may be the only refuge dedicated anywhere to the white-tailed deer, a particularly diminutive variety of it. An estimated 800 of the animals, weighing no more than a large dog, survive on a handful of Lower Keys islands. The refuge has achieved remarkable success in bringing back the Key deer population from the 1940s when their number was only an estimated twenty-seven to fifty animals. Hunting and development were well on their way to eliminating them. Key deer have rebounded so much so that driving too fast at night is hazardous to both man and beast. Nighttime collisions with autos on U.S. Highway 1 kill dozens of animals annually and result in considerable property damage.

▶ Key deer are most easily seen at dawn or dusk in the field at the far end of Key Deer Boulevard and along Watson Boulevard on No Name Key.

The refuge has a series of short nature trails that provide a good look at several sections. However, your best chance of finding Key deer is not on one of them but actually at a large vacant field adjacent to a housing development near the end of Key Deer Boulevard.

Nearest town: Big Pine Key
Start: Off Key Deer Boulevard and No Name Key
Difficulty: Easy
Trail surface: Natural surface and pavement
Seasons: Best walking conditions during winter months
Other trail users: Wildlife watchers
Canine compatibility: No pets
Land status: National wildlife refuge

Fees and permits: No admission charges
Schedule: The refuge is open from sunrise to sunset.
Maps: Available at visitor center and trails kiosk
Trail contacts: National Key Deer Refuge, 179 Key Deer Boulevard, Big Pine Key Plaza, Big Pine Key, FL 33043-0510; (305) 872-2239 or www.fws.gov/nationalkeydeer and http://nationalkeydeer.fws.gov

Finding the trailhead: Take US 1 to Big Pine Key. Turn north onto Key Deer Boulevard. The shopping center on the right contains the main refuge office. To find the trails, continue straight on Key Deer Boulevard. Look for the signs, all on the left, marking the trailheads. If you see a deer at any point along this drive and want to photograph it, pull well off the paved road, stop the engine, and feel free to get out. Don't make any sudden or threatening moves toward the animal. The deer are accustomed to people and may willingly pose for pictures.

Blue Hole

Distance: 0.2 mile out and back
Approximate hiking time: 15 minutes

GPS: N24 42.389' W 081 22.836'

The Hike

The well-marked trailhead is located about 3 miles north of the intersection with Watson Boulevard. The trail leads to an old, flooded rock quarry that contains at least one large alligator. Visitor facilities include an interpretive kiosk and an observation platform overlooking Blue Hole, a quarry made to supply material for the Overseas Highway. This quarry pool is the main freshwater source on Big Pine Key for wildlife.

Manillo Trail

Distance: 0.3-mile out and back
Approximate hiking time: 15 to 20 minutes

GPS: N24 42.571' W080 22.948'

The Hike

The parking area for this and the adjacent Watson Wildlife Trail are located about

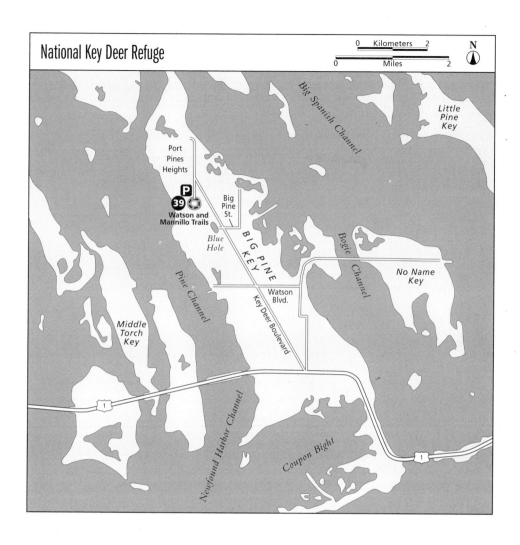

0.5 mile north of the Blue Hole. The Manillo Trail is wheelchair accessible due to its hard-packed gravel path that moves through a section of pine rocklands, a karst limestone landscape consisting of solution holes, saw palmetto, stunted slash pines, poisonwood trees, and the occasional silver or thatch palm. National Key Deer Refuge protects about 80 percent of the Keys' remaining pine rocklands.

Watson Wildlife Trail

Distance: 1.1-mile loop
Approximate hiking time: 30 minutes

GPS: N24 42.571' W080 22.948'

The Hike

This trailhead is adjacent to the start of the Manillo Trail and uses the same parking lot. The hike is named after an early refuge manager who helped bring the Key deer back from extinction. Like the Manillo Trail, it ventures into pine rocklands with slash pines (growing at their southernmost point) and numerous small poisonwood trees with their irritating sap. Deer trails going through the underbrush indicate the deer often roam through here. But to be honest, if seeing Key deer is your main objective, the following hike at Port Pine Heights is a surer bet.

Miles and Directions

0.0 Trail starts from the parking lot.

0.4 Trail begins to loop back.

0.6 Pass alligator hole.

1.1 Trail ends at parking lot.

Port Pine Heights

Distance: Each walk is less than a mile for each walk

Approximate hiking time: 15 to 20 minutes   **GPS:** N24 43.421' W081 23.279'

This housing development near the end of Key Deer Boulevard is perhaps the surest and easiest place to see Key deer close-up either early or late in the day. A large undeveloped tract between the road and most of the houses is where the deer typically graze in late afternoon. I have rarely been disappointed, but wild animals keep to their own schedule and their appearance is not guaranteed. If they are not here, look behind the Lion's Club located one more block away on Key Deer Boulevard.

Port Pine Heights has no defined trail, only a large vacant field to explore in your quest to sight a key deer. Walk slowly and carry a camera with a good telephoto lens. Some of these deer do seem to enjoy posing.

Key deer are classified as a subspecies of the Virginia white-tailed deer. It's believed their ancestors migrated to the Keys from the mainland thousands of years ago during the last glacial age when a land bridge existed. Rising water then isolated the herd. Key deer are genetically small and not stunted because of a limited food supply. No matter how much a Key deer eats—it is illegal for anyone to feed them—the animal will not grow larger than normal.

If, after all this, you're still deerless and it's not too late in the day, go back to the intersection with US 1 and take Wilder Road through the subdivisions and across the bridge to No Name Key. The deer are sometimes sighted here when they're scarce elsewhere, but being present at the proper time of day when the deer are out feeding is always the determining factor. Those times are typically the first hour after daybreak and an hour before sunset.

More Information

Local Information
Monroe County Tourist Development Council: www.fla-keys.com/lowerkeys.

Lodging
Accommodations are available in Big Pine Key and within Bahia Honda State Park.

Camping
Bahia Honda State Park has three different campgrounds with up to eighty sites.

Organizations
U.S. Fish and Wildlife Service Southeast Region: www.fws.gov/southeast.
Florida Keys National Wildlife Refuges: www.fws.gov/southeast/pubs/nkdgen.pdf.

THE BAT TOWER

After crossing the Seven Mile Bridge and continuing south to Key West, look for the tiny sign pointing to the famed bat tower. It's on the right, just past Sugarloaf Lodge on Sugarloaf Key near Mile Marker 17. The bat tower was one of the most ingenious failures in Keys' history. In 1929 an aspiring land developer who wanted to build a resort and casino here found his plans hampered by the huge mosquito population. He learned he might able to reduce the mosquito population if he could attract bats who would dine on the ferocious insects. He built an elaborate shingled tower about 35 feet tall for the bats to roost in and acquired an exotic bat bait as an attractant. But the bats never came—not one, ever. All the developer's plans folded, but the virginal bat tower still stands, a proud reminder of the days when Keys' life was a little zanier.

Hiker's Checklist

The "best" way to realize the importance of a good checklist is be on a wilderness trail about 15 miles from the trailhead and discover that you have forgotten an important item. The thing you forgot may be only an inconvenience, or it may be seriously important. A good checklist will help prevent your forgetting the things you need to make your hike safe and enjoyable.

This is only a suggested list. Base your list on the nature of the hike and your own personal needs. Items will vary depending on whether you are camping near your vehicle or backpacking to more remote campsites and staying out one or more nights. Remember, if you are carrying it on your back, select items judiciously. Weight is an important factor.

Check each item as you pack.

Day Hike Checklist

- ❏ Polarized sunglasses
- ❏ Waterproof sunblock
- ❏ Insect repellent
- ❏ Hat with full brim
- ❏ Compass and map of hiking area
- ❏ Fanny pack with snacks and two water bottles
- ❏ Cell phone in case of emergency
- ❏ Band-Aids for blisters
- ❏ Ankle support device in case of sprain
- ❏ First-aid kit with tweezers
- ❏ For thick mosquito country or prolonged sun exposure, lightweight long-sleeved shirt and long pants
- ❏ Raingear (dry clothes in case of rain)
- ❏ Ice chest with cold drinks in vehicle for your return

For Extended Hikes

All of the above plus the following items:

- ❏ GPS
- ❏ Flashlight with spare batteries
- ❏ Water-sterilizing tablets or portable water purifier
- ❏ Dusting powder for groin and feet
- ❏ Commercial rehydrating salts
- ❏ Antidiarrhetic
- ❏ Laxative (we all react differently)
- ❏ Aspirin

Index

Anhinga Trail, Everglades 50

Bahia Honda State Park 150
Bailey Tract, Ding Darling NWR 94
Bayshore Loop Trail, Everglades 64
Bear Lake Trail, Everglades 102
Blue Hole Trail, National Key Deer
    Refuge 155
Blue Trail, Oscar Scherer State Park 82
Boardwalk Trail: Corkscrew Swamp
    Sanctuary 35; Six Mile Cypress
    Slough Preserve 31
Bobcat Boardwalk, Everglades 66
Boylston Nature Trail, Myakka 19

Canopy Walkway, Myakka 19
Corbett (J. W.) Wildlife
    Management Area 73, 110
Corkscrew Swamp Sanctuary 35
Curry Hammock State Park 142
Cypress Swamp Boardwalk,
    Loxahatchee NWR 69

Dagny Johnson Key Largo Hammock
    Botanical State Park 120
Dickinson (Jonathan) State Park 105
Ding Darling National Wildlife
    Refuge 87
Duncan Memorial Trail, Florida
    Panther NWR 39
DuPuis Management Area 113

East Loop Trail, Jonathan Dickinson
    SP 105
Eco Pond Trail, Everglades 63
Everglades National Park: Hikes along
    the Main Road 48–68; Homestead
    to Flamingo Day Hikes 95–104

Fakahatchee Strand Preserve State
    Park 44
Florida Panther National Wildlife
    Refuge 39
Florida Trail Segment, Corbett WMA 110

Golden Orb Trail, Long Key State
    Park 137
Green Trail, Oscar Scherer State Park 86
Gumbo Limbo Trail, Everglades 53

Hammock Trail, Windley Key Fossil
    Reef SP 129
Hammock Walk, Key Largo Hammock
    Botanical SP 120
Highlands Hammock State Park 24
Hungryland Boardwalk and Trail,
    Corbett WMA 73

Indigo Trail, Ding Darling NWR 89

John Pennekamp Coral Reef State
    Park 124
Jonathan Dickinson State Park 105
J. W. Corbett Wildlife Management
    Area 73, 110

Layton Trail, Long Key State Park 137
Lignumvitae Key Botanical State
    Park 133
Long Key State Park 137
Loop Trails, DuPuis Management
    Area 113
Loxahatchee National Wildlife
    Refuge 69
Mahogany Hammock Trail,
    Everglades 58
Mangrove Trail, Pennekamp Coral Reef
    SP 124

Marathon Bridge Walk 147
Myakka River State Park 19

National Key Deer Refuge 155
Nature Boardwalk, Fakahatchee Strand
    Preserve SP 44
Nature Trail: Curry Hammock State
    Park 142; Lignumvitae Key
    Botanical SP 133; National Key
    Deer Refuge 155; Highlands
    Hammock State Park 24

Old Bridge Trail, Bahia Honda State
    Park 150
Old Seven Mile Bridge to Pigeon Key,
    Marathon Bridge Walk 147
Oscar Scherer State Park 78–86
Otter Cave Hammock Trail,
    Everglades 66

Pa-Hay-Okee Overlook Trail,
    Everglades 56
Pennekamp Coral Reef State Park 124
Pinelands Long Loop, Everglades 97
Pinelands Short Loop, Everglades 55

Red Trail, Oscar Scherer State Park 84
Royal Palm Hike, Everglades: Anhinga
    Trail 50; Gumbo Limbo Trail 53

Shark Valley, Everglades 66
Shell Mound Trail, Ding Darling
    NWR 92
Silver Palm Trail, Bahia Honda State
    Park 150
Six Mile Cypress Slough Preserve 31
Snake Bight/Rowdy Bend Trails,
    Everglades 100
Sunset Trail, Windley Key Fossil
    Reef SP 129

West Lake Mangrove Trail,
    Everglades 60
Wild Tamarind Trail, Pennekamp Coral
    Reef SP 124
Windley Key Fossil Reef Geological
    State Park 129

Yellow Trail, Oscar Scherer State
    Park 80

About the Author

Tim O'Keefe, a past president of the Florida Outdoor Writers Association and a member of the Florida Trail Association, has lived in the Orlando area since 1968. For almost three decades, his articles and photographs have appeared in numerous publications, including eight *National Geographic Society* books, *Men's Journal, National Geographic Traveler, Discovery Channel Online, Outside, Caribbean Travel & Life, Newsweek, Sport Diver,* the *New York Times,* and the *Chicago Tribune.*

His new Web site, www.floridawild lifeviewing.com, brings together all of his Florida outdoor experiences. His other love and expertise is the Caribbean, with his insights available at www.guidetocarib beanvacations.com (gtcv.com).

Tim was a major contributor to *National Geographic's Guide to Caribbean Family Vacations.* He also authored *Caribbean Hiking; The Spicy Camp Cook Book; Seasonal Guide to the Natural Year: Florida with Georgia and Alabama Coasts; Great Adventures in Florida; Manatees, Our Vanishing Mermaids; Sea Turtles, The Watcher's Guide: Fish and Dive the Caribbean* and *Fish and Dive Florida & The Keys* (both with Larry Larsen); *Diving to Adventure;* and the AAA's *A Photo Journey to Central Florida.*

Tim's work has won more than fifty regional and national awards. *The Spicy Camp Cook Book* and *Seasonal Guide to the Natural Year: Florida with Georgia and Alabama Coasts* were named "Best Book" by the Florida Outdoor Writers Association. Tim has published more than 10,000 photographs worldwide.

Visit the premier outdoor online community ...

FALCON GUIDES®

LOGIN | CREATE AN ACCOUNT   Search

HOME   ABOUT US   CONTACT US   BOOKS   BLOGS   PHOTOS   TRAIL FINDER

4 of 6

The Art of Cycling
Bicycling In Traffic
Part one: Beyond the Vehicular Cycling Principle

HIKING WITH KIDS

HAPPY TRAILS Hiking in the Great Outdoors is a simple gift we all can give our children, grandchildren, and young friends. Unlike playing music, writing poetry, painting pictures, or other activities that also can fill your soul, hiking does not require any special skill. All you need to do is put one foot in front of the other in the outdoors, repeatedly. And breathe deeply.

LEARN MORE

FEATURED NEW BOOK

SCAVENGER HIKE ADVENTURES: GREAT SMOKY MOUNTAINS NATIONAL PARK

A Totally New Interactive Hiking Guide

Introducing a brand new genre of hiking guide. Readers follow clues to find over 200 hidden natural and historic treasures on as many as 14 easy, moderate, and extreme hikes national parks. Follow the clues and find such things as a tree clawed open by a bear searching for food, an ancient Indian footpath, the remains of an old Model T Ford deep in the forest, and over 200 other unusual treasures.

CLICK HERE TO FIND OUT MORE

RECENT BLOG POSTS

- A Dry River
- Stat-mongering -- Look Out!
- Lizard Man
- Tropical Tip of Texas
- Lions And Snakes and Bears..Oh My! "Don's PCT Update"
- Bikin' in C'ville
- The Red Store
- Journey to Idyllwild
- A Spring Quandary
- Whew!! Rocky Mountain book is printed I'm going camping!!

more

EXPERT BLOGS

- Arrowleaf Balsamroot—Another
  By: Bert Gildart
- Splitter camps #2
  By: Katie Brown
- Splitter camp
  By: Katie Brown
- Alaska Boating Adventure

outfit your mind™

- Chris Sharma
- Beth Rodden
- Dean Potter
- Jason Kehl
- Josh Wharton
- Steph Davis

falcon.com